KRAFT

®

best-ever GRILLING

Recipe Collection

Somehow a meal served hot off the grill transforms an ordinary dinner into a spectacular one, with little effort required by the cook. To help you get started, turn to *Kraft Best-Ever Grilling Recipe Collection*. Along with inspired ideas for grilled meats, poultry and fish, you'll find recipes for tempting appetizers, refreshing beverages, savory side dishes and delectable desserts. Plus, you'll discover party menus, potluck dishes and tips for making your whole meal come together.

CONTENTS

© 2001 KF Holdings and Meredith Corporation
All rights reserved.
Produced by Meredith® Books,
1716 Locust St., Des Moines, IA 50309-3023.
ISBN: 0-696-21373-7 Printed in the United States of America.

Shown on front cover: Meat Lover's Steak (recipe, page 6)

Marinated Pork Chops
with Grilled Vegetables
(recipe, page 15)

BACKYARD STEAK AND CHOP HOUSE

The irresistible aroma of juicy meats sizzling on your grill will draw your family and friends to the dinner table. Whether it is Meat Lover's Steak, Marinated Pork Chops with Grilled Vegetables, Savory Feta Burgers or Cheezy Dogs that pleases your palate, you'll find ideas for all sorts of hot-off-the-grill dinners. So head for the backyard and fire up the grill.

Meat *Lover's* Steak

(Photo on front cover.)

Prep time: 5 minutes   Grilling time: 20 minutes

Makes 4 to 6 servings

1½ **pounds beef steak, 1 inch thick**
1   **clove garlic, halved**
1   **large red onion, cut into ¼-inch slices**
1   **cup KRAFT Original Barbecue Sauce *or***
     KRAFT THICK 'N SPICY Barbecue Sauce

Rub both sides of steak with halved garlic clove.

Place steak and onion on greased grill over medium coals.

Grill, uncovered, about 20 minutes or until medium doneness (160°F), brushing steak and onion frequently with barbecue sauce and turning occasionally. Serve with grilled vegetables (tip, page 58), if desired.

Try Broiling

To broil rather than grill Meat Lover's Steak, place steak and onion on greased rack of broiler pan 3 to 4 inches from heat. Broil about 20 minutes or until done, brushing steak and onion frequently with barbecue sauce and turning occasionally.

Grilled Steak Salad

Prep time: 10 minutes plus marinating   Grilling time: 15 minutes

Makes 4 servings

1½ cups SEVEN SEAS VIVA Italian Dressing,
      divided
1   pound boneless beef sirloin steak
½   pound new potatoes, cut into quarters
1   package (10 ounces) salad greens
1   cup tomato wedges
½   cup slivered red onion

Place steak in glass baking dish. Pour 1 cup of the dressing over steak; cover. Refrigerate 4 hours or overnight to marinate. Drain, discarding dressing.

Place potatoes in double layer of heavy-duty foil to form pouch; top with remaining ½ cup dressing. Place potato pouch and steak on greased grill over medium coals.

Grill 12 to 15 minutes or until medium doneness (160°F), turning occasionally. Cool slightly; carve steak across grain into thin strips. Toss greens, tomato, onion, steak strips and potatoes.

Easy Serve-Along

Take advantage of the grill for a bread accompaniment for Grilled Steak Salad. Butter French bread slices and grill next to the meat.

Savory Steak and Spinach Salad

Prep time: 10 minutes plus marinating   Grilling time: 12 minutes

Makes 4 servings

1   cup Robust Italian Dressing (recipe, page 104), divided
1   pound beef sirloin steak, ½ to ¾ inch thick
8   cups torn spinach
1   cup sliced mushrooms
1   large tomato, cut into wedges
½   cup red onion rings

Pour ½ cup of the dressing over steak; cover. Refrigerate at least 1 hour to marinate. Drain, discarding dressing.

Place steak on greased grill over medium coals.

Grill 5 to 6 minutes on each side or until medium doneness (160°F). Cool slightly; carve steak across grain into thin slices.

Toss spinach, mushrooms, tomato and onion with remaining ½ cup dressing. Arrange steak slices over salad.

KRAFT® BBQ Beef *Fajitas*

Prep time: 10 minutes plus marinating   Grilling time: 14 minutes

Makes 4 servings

1   **bottle (18 ounces) KRAFT Original Barbecue Sauce, divided**
¼   **cup lemon *or* lime juice**
¼   **cup water**
1   **pound beef flank steak**
1   ***each* medium green and red pepper, cut lengthwise into quarters**
1   **medium red onion, sliced**
4   **flour tortillas (10 inch) *or* 8 flour tortillas (6 inch)**

Mix 1 cup of the barbecue sauce, lemon juice and water in small bowl. Set aside. Score steak by making shallow cuts in the surface on both sides. Place steak in glass baking dish. Pour barbecue sauce mixture over steak; cover. Refrigerate several hours or overnight to marinate. Drain, discarding marinade.

Place steak, peppers and onion on greased grill over medium coals. Grill 12 to 14 minutes or until medium doneness (160°F), turning and brushing occasionally with additional barbecue sauce.

Cool slightly; carve steak across grain into thin slices. Cut peppers into thin slices. Place meat and vegetables on center of each tortilla; fold up sides to enclose filling. Garnish with lemon wedges. Serve with additional barbecue sauce.

BBQ *Grilled* Steak Wraps

Prep time: 15 minutes   Grilling time: 12 minutes

Makes 4

1   **pound beef skirt steak**
2   **medium green *or* red peppers, quartered**
1   **medium onion, sliced**
1   **cup KRAFT Steakhouse Style Barbecue Sauce *or* KRAFT Original Barbecue Sauce**
4   **flour tortillas (10 inch) *or* 8 flour tortillas (6 inch)**

Place steak and vegetables on greased grill over medium coals.

Grill steak 5 to 6 minutes on each side or until medium doneness (160°F) and vegetables 4 to 5 minutes on each side, brushing each frequently with barbecue sauce.

Cool slightly; slice steak and vegetables into thin strips. Divide meat and vegetables among tortillas; roll up. Serve with additional barbecue sauce and lime wedges, if desired.

Grilled Pork Tenderloin with *Corn-Pepper* Relish

Prep time: 10 minutes   Grilling time: 15 minutes

Makes 8 servings

2 pork tenderloins (10 to 12 ounces *each)*
1 cup prepared GOOD SEASONS Zesty Italian *or* Italian Salad Dressing, divided
1 can (15 ounces) black beans, drained, rinsed
1 can (10 ounces) whole kernel corn, drained
1 red pepper, chopped

Place pork on greased grill over medium coals. Grill 12 to 15 minutes or until cooked through (170°F), turning every 4 minutes and brushing with ½ cup of the dressing. Cut into ½-inch slices.

Mix beans, corn, red pepper and remaining ½ cup dressing. Serve with pork.

Olive Oil Hints

Keep olive oil at its peak by storing it in a cool, dark place where it will last for up to a year. When chilling GOOD SEASONS Salad Dressing Mix prepared with olive oil, the oil may solidify and the dressing may be too thick to pour immediately. This won't affect the flavor. Simply let the dressing stand at room temperature for 10 to 15 minutes, shake or mix it and serve.

Marinated Pork Chops with Grilled Vegetables

(Photo on pages 4–5.)

Prep time: 5 minutes plus marinating   Grilling time: 16 minutes

Makes 4 servings

1   cup KRAFT House Italian Dressing
¼   cup Dijon mustard
4   bone-in *or* boneless pork chops, ½ inch
     thick
     Red and yellow peppers, cut
       lengthwise into wedges
     Diagonally sliced zucchini

Mix dressing and mustard. Reserve ½ cup of the dressing mixture. Pierce both sides of each chop several times with fork. Pour remaining dressing mixture over chops in glass baking dish or zipper-style plastic bag; cover.

Refrigerate 15 minutes to marinate. Drain, discarding marinade.

Place chops and vegetables on grill over medium coals. Grill 7 to 8 minutes on each side or until pork is cooked through (170°F), brushing occasionally with reserved ½ cup dressing mixture.

How to Marinate Foods

- Marinate foods in a glass or plastic dish instead of a metal container, because acid in a marinade may pit the container and add an off-flavor to the marinade.

- If you marinate in a plastic bag, use a heavy-duty bag and set it in a bowl just in case the bag leaks.

- Marinate foods in the refrigerator. Don't let them stand at room temperature.

- Marinades are not reusable. Discard any leftover marinade.

BULL'S-EYE® Grilled BBQ *Pork Chop* Sandwiches

Prep time: 5 minutes   Grilling time: 16 minutes

Makes 4

4 boneless pork chops, ½ inch thick
1 bottle (18 ounces) BULL'S-EYE Original
   Barbecue Sauce
4 large tomato slices
4 onion slices
4 Kaiser rolls *or* onion rolls
   Leaf lettuce

Place chops on grill over medium coals. Brush with barbecue sauce. Grill 6 to 8 minutes on each side or until cooked through (170°F), brushing occasionally with barbecue sauce.

Place tomato and onion on grill during last 4 minutes of grilling time, turning and brushing occasionally with barbecue sauce.

Spread rolls with barbecue sauce. Fill with lettuce, chops, tomato and onion.

Tiger-Striped Cheeseburgers

Prep time: 15 minutes   Grilling time: 18 minutes

Makes 4

1 **pound ground beef**
2 **KRAFT DELI DELUXE Process American Cheese Slices, each slice cut into 6 strips**
4 **Kaiser rolls *or* hamburger buns, split, toasted**
   Lettuce leaves

Shape meat into 4 patties.

Place patties on grill over medium coals. Grill 7 to 9 minutes on each side or until cooked through (160°F).

Top each patty with 3 process cheese food strips to resemble stripes. Continue grilling until process cheese begins to melt. Fill rolls with lettuce and cheeseburgers.

BBQ *Cheeseburgers*

Prep time: 10 minutes   Grilling time: 18 minutes

Makes 4

1   **pound ground beef**
2   **tablespoons KRAFT Original Barbecue Sauce**
4   **VELVEETA Pasteurized Prepared Cheese Product Slices**
4   **hamburger buns *or* Kaiser rolls, split, toasted**
    Lettuce leaves
    Tomato slices

Mix meat and barbecue sauce. Shape into 4 patties.

Place patties on greased grill over medium coals. Grill 7 to 9 minutes on each side or until cooked through (160°F), brushing occasionally with additional barbecue sauce.

Top each patty with 1 prepared cheese product slice. Continue grilling until prepared cheese product begins to melt. Fill buns with cheeseburgers. Top with additional barbecue sauce, lettuce and tomato slices.

Taco Cheeseburger
(recipe, opposite)

Taco Cheeseburgers

Prep time: 10 minutes   Grilling time: 18 minutes

Makes 4

1   **pound ground beef**
1   **package (1¼ ounces) TACO BELL HOME ORIGINALS Taco Seasoning Mix**
8   **KRAFT DELI DELUXE Process American Cheese Slices**
4   **Kaiser rolls *or* hamburger buns, split, toasted**
    Lettuce leaves
    TACO BELL HOME ORIGINALS Thick 'N Chunky Salsa

Mix meat and seasoning mix. Shape into 4 patties.

Place patties on grill over medium coals. Grill 7 to 9 minutes on each side or until cooked through (160°F).

Top each patty with 2 process cheese slices; continue grilling until process cheese begins to melt. Fill rolls with lettuce and cheeseburgers; top with salsa.

TACO BELL and HOME ORIGINALS are registered trademarks owned and licensed by Taco Bell Corp.

Zesty Burgers

Prep time: 5 minutes   Grilling time: 18 minutes

Makes 4

1½   **pounds ground beef**
1   **envelope GOOD SEASONS Zesty Italian *or* Italian Salad Dressing Mix**

Mix meat and salad dressing mix. Shape into 4 patties.

Place patties on greased grill over medium coals. Grill 7 to 9 minutes on each side or until cooked through (160°F).

BULL'S-EYE® BBQ *Burgers*

Prep time: 5 minutes   Grilling time: 18 minutes

Makes 6

1½ **pounds ground beef**
    BULL'S-EYE Original Barbecue Sauce
6 **onion slices**
6 **hamburger buns, split, toasted**
    Leaf lettuce
    Tomato slices

Mix meat and 2 tablespoons barbecue sauce. Shape into 6 patties.

Place patties on greased grill over medium coals. Grill 7 to 9 minutes on each side or until cooked through (160°F), brushing occasionally with barbecue sauce. Place onions on grill during last 4 minutes of grilling time, turning once and brushing with barbecue sauce.

Spread buns with barbecue sauce. Fill with lettuce, tomato, burgers and onions.

How to Toast Buns

It's easy to toast buns or Kaiser rolls on the grill alongside burgers. Place buns on grill during the last minute of grilling time. Watch carefully so the buns don't burn.

All American *Deluxe* Cheeseburgers

Prep time: 10 minutes   Grilling time: 18 minutes

Makes 4

1   **pound ground beef**
8   **KRAFT DELI DELUXE Process American Cheese Slices**
2   **tablespoons KRAFT Thousand Island Dressing**
2   **tablespoons KRAFT Mayo Real Mayonnaise**
4   **Kaiser rolls *or* hamburger buns, split, toasted**
    Red onion and tomato slices
    CLAUSSEN Classic Dill Super Slices for Burgers
    Lettuce

Shape meat into 4 patties. Place patties on grill over medium coals. Grill 7 to 9 minutes on each side or until cooked through (160°F).

Top each patty with 2 process cheese slices. Continue grilling until process cheese begins to melt.

Mix dressing and mayo in small bowl. Spread 1 tablespoon dressing mixture on each roll bottom. Fill rolls with onion, cheeseburgers, pickle, tomato and lettuce.

Savory Feta Burgers

Prep time: 10 minutes   Grilling time: 18 minutes

Makes 4

1   **pound ground beef**
1   **package (8 ounces) ATHENOS Feta Cheese with Basil & Tomato, divided**
¼   **teaspoon fennel seed, crushed (optional)**
⅛   **teaspoon ground black pepper**

Mix meat, ½ of the cheese, crumbled, and seasonings. Shape into 4 patties.

Place patties on grill over medium coals. Grill 7 to 9 minutes on each side or until cooked through (160°F). Cut remaining cheese into 4 slices; place on top of burgers. Continue grilling until cheese begins to melt.

Serve on Kaiser rolls with lettuce, tomato and onion slices, if desired.

Savory Feta Lamb Burgers

For a delicious change of pace, prepare Savory Feta Burgers as directed, substituting ground lamb for half or all of the ground beef.

Best *Meatless* Burgers

Prep time: 5 minutes   Grilling time: 8 minutes

Makes 4

1   **package (10 ounces) frozen
     BOCA BURGER Meatless Burgers**
4   **Kaiser rolls, split, toasted
     PHILADELPHIA Chive & Onion Cream
     Cheese
     CLAUSSEN Burger Slices**

Place frozen patties on grill over hot coals. Grill 4 minutes on each side or until thoroughly heated.

Spread cut surfaces of rolls with cream cheese. Fill with patties and pickle slices.

Great Substitute

Prepare Best Meatless Burgers as directed, substituting PHILADELPHIA Garden Vegetable Cream Cheese for Chive & Onion Cream Cheese.

burger *ideas*

*Who doesn't love a burger? Start with a pound
of ground meat and add pizzazz with these easy ideas.*

Taco Burgers

Mix 1 package
(1¼ ounces)
TACO BELL
HOME ORIGINALS
Taco Seasoning Mix
into 1 pound ground
beef. Form into
patties and grill over
medium coals until
cooked through
(160°F). Top with
KRAFT Four Cheese
Mexican Style
Shredded Cheese;
grill until melted.
Serve with lettuce
and TACO BELL
HOME ORIGINALS
Thick 'N Chunky
Salsa, if desired.

**Garlic Herb
Turkey Burgers**

Mix 1 envelope
GOOD SEASONS
Garlic & Herb
Salad Dressing
Mix into 1 pound
ground turkey or
beef. Form into
patties and grill
over medium coals
until cooked through
(165°F). Serve
with CLAUSSEN
Burger Slices and
tomato slices.

**Bacon
Cheeseburgers**

Cook slices of
OSCAR MAYER
Bacon alongside
burgers on the grill
until bacon is crisp.
Break slices in half.
Top each burger
with 2 KRAFT
DELI DELUXE Process
American Cheese
Slices; grill until
process cheese
begins to melt. Serve
with KRAFT Ranch
Dressing and
crisscross bacon
pieces over burgers.

Pretzel Cheese Dogs

Prep time: 5 minutes   Grilling time: 8 minutes

OSCAR MAYER Cheese Dogs *or* Beef Franks
Hot dog buns
Honey mustard *or* pretzel dip
Crumbled pretzels

Grill cheese dogs until thoroughly heated (160°F), turning frequently.

Place cheese dogs in buns; top with honey mustard and pretzels.

Feisty *Mustard* Topped Franks

Prep time: 10 minutes   Grilling time: 10 minutes

Makes 8

2   **CLAUSSEN Whole Kosher Dill Pickles,**
    chopped (about ½ cup)
1   **can (4 ounces) chopped green chilies,**
    drained
2   **tablespoons chopped onion**
2   **tablespoons mustard**
8   **OSCAR MAYER Beef Franks *or* Wieners**
8   **hot dog buns**

Mix pickles, chilies, onion and mustard.

Grill franks until thoroughly heated (160°F), turning occasionally.

Place franks in buns; top with pickle mixture.

Make-Ahead Directions

The pickle mixture for Feisty Mustard Topped Franks can be made a day ahead. Refrigerate it until ready to serve.

Pepper Pot Hot Dogs

Prep time: 5 minutes   Grilling time: 15 minutes

Makes 8

2   **peppers (red, green *or* yellow), cut into strips**
1   **small onion, sliced**
¼   **cup KRAFT Italian Dressing**
8   **OSCAR MAYER Beef Franks *or* Wieners**
8   **hot dog buns**

Place peppers, onion and dressing in heavy-duty foil bag or foil pouch. Heat on grill 15 minutes or until vegetables are tender, turning bag occasionally.

Grill franks until thoroughly heated (160°F), turning occasionally.

Place franks in buns; top with pepper mixture.

Caesar Cheese Dogs

Prep time: 5 minutes   *Grilling time: 8 minutes*

OSCAR MAYER Cheese Dogs *or* Beef Franks
Hot dog buns, split, toasted
CLAUSSEN Bread 'N Butter Sandwich Slices *or* Pickle Chips
Chopped tomato
KRAFT Caesar Ranch Dressing

Grill cheese hot dogs until thoroughly heated (160°F), turning frequently.

Serve cheese dogs in buns with pickles and tomato. Drizzle with dressing.

Franks in *Broccoli Slaw* Nests

Prep time: 5 minutes   Grilling time: 10 minutes

Makes 8

2   **cups broccoli slaw *or* cole slaw blend**
½   **cup MIRACLE WHIP Salad Dressing**
¼   **cup chopped red onion**
8   **OSCAR MAYER Beef Franks *or* Wieners**
8   **hot dog buns**

Mix slaw, salad dressing and onion.

Grill franks until thoroughly heated (160°F), turning occasionally.

Spoon about ¼ cup slaw mixture into each bun; top with frank.

Dress Up Beans

Give the all-time favorite combo of franks and beans a new twist. Stir some chopped pepper into canned or deli baked beans.

Cheezy Dogs

Prep time: 5 minutes   Grilling time: 6 minutes

Makes 8

1 package (16 ounces) OSCAR MAYER
Bun-Length Beef Franks *or* Wieners
8 hot dog buns
1 cup CHEEZ WHIZ Cheese Dip,
microwaved as directed on label

Grill franks until thoroughly heated (160°F), turning occasionally.

Place franks in buns. Drizzle about 2 tablespoons cheese dip over each frank.

Hot Dog Wrap *Olé*

Prep time: 5 minutes   Grilling time: 10 minutes

Makes 8

8   OSCAR MAYER Beef Franks *or* Wieners
8   flour tortillas (6 to 8 inch), warmed
8   KRAFT Mexican *or* American Singles
**   TACO BELL HOME ORIGINALS Thick 'N**
**   Chunky Salsa**
Torn lettuce

Grill franks until thoroughly heated (160°F), turning occasionally.

Top each tortilla with 1 Singles, grilled frank, salsa and lettuce; fold.

TACO BELL and HOME ORIGINALS are registered trademarks owned and licensed by Taco Bell Corp.

Dynamite Dogs

Prep time: 5 minutes   Grilling time: 8 minutes

**OSCAR MAYER Cheese Dogs *or* Beef
  Franks**
Hot dog buns
**CLAUSSEN Bread 'N Butter Sandwich
  Slices *or* Pickle Chips**
**BULL'S-EYE Spicy Hot Barbecue Sauce *or*
  Original Barbecue Sauce**

Grill cheese dogs until thoroughly heated
(160°F), turning frequently.

Serve in buns with pickle slices and
barbecue sauce.

hot dog *ideas*

*Whatever you call 'em—hot dogs, franks or wieners—
call 'em quick to fix and divine to dig into. Try these
new variations on the longtime favorite.*

Tex-Mex Dogs

Mix ½ cup CLAUSSEN
Sweet Pickle Relish;
1 can (4 ounces)
chopped green chilies,
drained; 2 tablespoons
chopped onion and
2 tablespoons mustard.
Spoon over franks.

California Dogs

Top franks with
shredded lettuce,
chopped tomatoes and
chopped onion; drizzle
with KRAFT Russian
Dressing.

Garden-Vegetable Franks

Mix 1 small tomato,
chopped; ½ cucumber,
finely chopped;
3 radishes, sliced and
cut in half; and
2 green onions, sliced
with ½ cup KRAFT
Ranch Dressing. Spoon
over franks.

Texas Dogs

Top franks with a
little mustard. Spoon
on heated leftover
or canned chili and
sprinkle with chopped
onion.

Pizza Dogs

Top franks with heated
pizza sauce; sprinkle
with KRAFT Shredded
Low-Moisture Part-Skim
Mozzarella Cheese.

Italian Dogs

Top franks with
sautéed onions and
peppers; spoon on
heated pasta sauce.

Sauerkraut Dogs

Top franks with
mustard and rinsed
and drained
sauerkraut.

Grilled Garlicky Chicken
Breasts (recipe, page 42)
and grilled vegetables (tip,
page 58)

POULTRY AND SEAFOOD ON THE GRILL

When the weather heats up and you're looking for a meal that is refreshing and satisfying, plan to serve one of these delicious grilled poultry or seafood dishes. You can't go wrong with this selection of recipes including Tangy Grilled Chicken Kabobs, Grilled Italian Shrimp and Zesty Grilled Turkey Burgers, as well as all-purpose marinades and barbecue sauces you can use to improvise your own creations.

Grilled *Garlicky* Chicken Breasts

(Photo on pages 40–41.)

Prep time: 5 minutes   Grilling time: 15 minutes

Makes 6 servings

1	envelope **GOOD SEASONS Roasted Garlic** *or* **Italian Salad Dressing Mix**
½	cup **KRAFT 100% Grated Parmesan Cheese**
6	**boneless skinless chicken breast halves (about 2 pounds)**

Mix salad dressing mix and cheese.

Moisten chicken in water; dip in dressing mixture.

Place chicken on greased grill over medium coals. Grill 12 to 15 minutes or until cooked through (160°F), turning once.

Grill Once, Eat Twice

Plan ahead and take advantage of your hot grill. Grill up a double batch of tonight's chicken breasts or steak, and transform them into tomorrow night's chef's salad or beef and cheese sandwiches.

Sassy Southern Chicken

Prep time: 10 minutes plus marinating   Grilling time: 15 minutes

Makes 4 servings

3 tablespoons *each* cider vinegar and
   whiskey
1 envelope GOOD SEASONS Honey French
   Salad Dressing Mix
½ cup oil
1 pound boneless skinless chicken breast
   halves

Mix all ingredients except chicken in small bowl until well blended.

Pour dressing mixture over chicken in glass baking dish; cover. Refrigerate 1 hour to marinate. Drain, discarding marinade.

Place chicken on greased grill over medium coals. Grill 12 to 15 minutes or until cooked through (160°F), turning once.

Caribbean *Jerk* Chicken

Prep time: 10 minutes plus marinating   Grilling or Broiling time: 45 minutes

Makes 6 to 8 servings

1   **envelope GOOD SEASONS Italian Salad Dressing Mix**

2   **tablespoons *each* brown sugar, oil and soy sauce**

1   **teaspoon *each* ground cinnamon and thyme**

½   **teaspoon ground red pepper**

2½   **pounds chicken pieces**

Mix all ingredients except chicken in small bowl until well blended.

Pour dressing mixture over chicken in glass baking dish; cover. Refrigerate 1 hour to marinate. Drain, discarding marinade.

Place on greased grill over medium coals or on rack of broiler pan 5 to 7 inches from heat. Grill or broil 40 to 45 minutes or until cooked through (160°F), turning frequently.

Citrus Barbecued Chicken Breasts

Prep time: 15 minutes plus marinating   Grilling time: 15 minutes

Makes 6 servings

1½ **cups KRAFT Original Barbecue Sauce or KRAFT THICK 'N SPICY Honey Barbecue Sauce**

⅓ **cup orange juice**

1 **tablespoon grated orange peel**

6 **boneless skinless chicken breast halves (about 2 pounds)**

Mix barbecue sauce, orange juice and peel. Reserve ½ cup sauce mixture. Pour remaining sauce mixture into glass baking dish. Add chicken to sauce mixture; turn to coat well. Cover. Refrigerate 30 minutes to marinate. Drain, discarding marinade.

Place chicken on greased grill over medium coals. Grill 12 to 15 minutes or until cooked through (160°F), turning and brushing with reserved ½ cup sauce mixture halfway through grilling time.

Marinated Shish Kabobs
(recipe, opposite) and Spicy
Vegetable Couscous (recipe,
page 117)

Marinated *Shish* Kabobs

Prep time: 15 minutes plus marinating   Grilling time: 15 minutes

Makes 6 servings

¾ **cup Mediterranean Vinaigrette (recipe below) *or* prepared Italian dressing**

1¼ **pounds boneless skinless chicken breasts *or* beef tenderloin, cut into 1½-inch chunks**

2 **cups assorted vegetables (such as pepper chunks, zucchini slices and onion wedges)**

Pour dressing over chicken and vegetables in large zipper-style plastic bag; seal bag. Refrigerate 2 hours or overnight to marinate, turning occasionally.

Thread chicken and vegetables on 6 skewers.

Place kabobs on greased grill over medium coals. Grill 12 to 15 minutes or until chicken is cooked through (160°F), turning once. Serve with Spicy Vegetable Couscous (recipe, page 117) and garnish with fresh herbs.

Mediterranean Vinaigrette

Place 3 tablespoons red wine vinegar; 2 cloves garlic, peeled; 2 teaspoons sugar; 1 teaspoon Dijon mustard; ¾ teaspoon salt and ¼ teaspoon pepper in blender container. Cover. Blend until smooth.

Add ⅔ cup olive oil; cover. Blend 15 seconds or until well mixed and slightly opaque. Serve over salad greens or in recipes calling for prepared oil-based dressings. Makes ¾ cup.

Tangy Grilled Chicken Kabobs

Prep time: 10 minutes plus marinating   Grilling time: 15 minutes

Makes 6 servings

1 cup MIRACLE WHIP **Salad Dressing**
1 envelope GOOD SEASONS **Italian Salad Dressing Mix**
2 tablespoons *each* **vinegar and water**
1½ **pounds boneless skinless chicken breast halves *or* boneless beef sirloin steak, cut into 1½-inch pieces
Assorted fresh vegetables (such as cherry tomatoes and cut-up red onion, peppers and zucchini)**

Mix salad dressing, salad dressing mix, vinegar and water. Reserve ½ cup salad dressing mixture.

Arrange chicken and vegetables on wooden skewers. Place kabobs in glass baking dish. Pour remaining salad dressing mixture over kabobs; cover. Refrigerate 30 minutes to marinate. Drain, discarding marinade.

Place kabobs on greased grill over medium coals. Grill 12 to 15 minutes or until chicken is cooked through (160°F), turning once. Serve with reserved ½ cup salad dressing mixture.

Grilled *Italian* Chicken Breasts

Prep time: 10 minutes   Grilling time: 15 minutes

Makes 6 servings

½ **cup KRAFT 100% Grated Parmesan Cheese**

¼ **cup dry bread crumbs**

1 **teaspoon *each* dried oregano leaves and parsley flakes**

¼ **teaspoon *each* paprika, salt and pepper**

6 **boneless skinless chicken breast halves (about 2 pounds)**

2 **tablespoons butter *or* margarine, melted**

Mix cheese, bread crumbs and seasonings.

Dip chicken in butter; coat with cheese mixture.

Place chicken on greased grill over medium coals. Grill 12 to 15 minutes or until cooked through (160°F), turning occasionally.

49

Bistro Chicken with Parmesan

Prep time: 25 minutes   Grilling time: 15 minutes

Makes 4 servings

2   boneless skinless chicken breast halves
2   cups cooked penne *or* rotini pasta
1   cup quartered cherry tomatoes
1   cup DI GIORNO Shredded Parmesan Cheese
½   cup prepared GOOD SEASONS Gourmet Caesar *or* Italian Salad Dressing
⅓   cup lightly packed fresh basil leaves, cut into strips
¼   cup *each* chopped red onion and sun-dried tomatoes, drained, chopped

Place chicken on greased grill over medium coals. Grill 12 to 15 minutes or until cooked through (160°F), turning once. Cool chicken slightly; cut into ¼-inch slices.

Mix chicken and remaining ingredients. Serve warm or chilled.

Grilled Chicken
Caesar Salad
(recipe, opposite)
and Grilled Bread
(recipe, page 116)

Grilled Chicken *Caesar* Salad

Prep time: 15 minutes plus marinating   Grilling time: 15 minutes

Makes 4 servings

1   **envelope GOOD SEASONS Gourmet
    Caesar *or* Italian Salad Dressing Mix**
¼   **cup lemon juice**
4   **boneless skinless chicken breast halves
    (about 1¼ pounds)**
6   **cups torn romaine lettuce**
1   **cup croutons**
½   **cup DI GIORNO Shredded Parmesan
    Cheese**

Prepare salad dressing mix as directed on envelope, except substitute lemon juice for vinegar. Reserve ½ cup of the dressing mixture.

Pour remaining dressing mixture over chicken in glass baking dish; cover. Refrigerate 1 hour to marinate. Drain, discarding marinade.

Place chicken on greased grill over medium coals. Grill 12 to 15 minutes or until cooked through (160°F), turning once. Cool slightly; cut into slices.

Toss lettuce, croutons and cheese with reserved ½ cup dressing. Arrange chicken slices over salad.

Asian Chicken with Peanut Slaw

Prep time: 15 minutes   Grilling time: 15 minutes

Makes 4 servings

4   **boneless skinless chicken breast halves
    (about 1¼ pounds)**
1   **cup prepared GOOD SEASONS Oriental
    Sesame Salad Dressing, divided**
2   **cups finely shredded green cabbage**
1   **medium carrot, shredded**
½   **cup roasted peanuts**

Place chicken on greased grill over medium coals. Grill 12 to 15 minutes or until cooked through (160°F), turning once and brushing with ½ cup of the dressing.

Toss cabbage, carrot, peanuts and remaining ½ cup dressing. Serve with chicken.

Sweet Orange and Chicken Salad

Prep time: 10 minutes   Grilling time: 15 minutes

Makes 6 servings

1 bottle (8 ounces) KRAFT CATALINA
   Dressing *or* KRAFT FREE CATALINA Fat
   Free Dressing, divided
4 boneless skinless chicken breast halves
   (about 1¼ pounds)
1 *each* red, yellow and green pepper,
   quartered
1 package (10 ounces) salad greens
2 oranges, peeled, sectioned
1 tablespoon toasted sesame seed

Brush ½ cup of the dressing on chicken
and peppers.

Place chicken and peppers on greased grill
over medium coals. Grill 12 to 15 minutes
or until chicken is cooked through (160°F),
turning once. Cool slightly; slice chicken
diagonally into strips. Cut peppers into
thin strips.

Toss chicken, peppers, greens, oranges
and remaining dressing. Sprinkle with
sesame seed.

CATALINA® Chicken *Wings*

Prep time: 5 minutes plus marinating   Grilling time: 20 minutes

Makes about 6 dozen

1   **bottle (16 ounces) KRAFT CATALINA Dressing**
½   **cup soy sauce**
5   **pounds chicken wings, separated at joints, tips discarded, and/or chicken drummettes**

Mix dressing and soy sauce; reserve ½ cup of the dressing mixture.

Pour remaining dressing mixture over chicken in large zipper-style plastic bags; seal bags. Refrigerate several hours or overnight to marinate. Drain, discarding marinade.

Place chicken on greased grill over medium coals. Grill 20 minutes or until cooked through (160°F), turning once and brushing occasionally with reserved ½ cup dressing mixture. Serve with blue cheese dressing sprinkled with cracked pepper.

Sizzlin' Fajitas

Prep time: 10 minutes plus refrigerating   Grilling time: 15 minutes

Makes 8 servings

1   cup BREAKSTONE'S *or* KNUDSEN Sour Cream
3   tablespoons chopped fresh cilantro
½   teaspoon lime juice
1¼ pounds boneless skinless chicken breast halves, cut into strips
1   large red onion, cut into thin wedges
1   green pepper, cut into chunks
1   tablespoon oil
8   flour tortillas (6 to 8 inch)
    TACO BELL HOME ORIGINALS Thick 'N Chunky Salsa

Mix sour cream, cilantro and lime juice. Refrigerate.

Arrange chicken, onion and green pepper on skewers; brush with oil. Place kabobs on greased grill over medium coals. Grill 12 to 15 minutes or until chicken is cooked through (160°F), turning once. Warm tortillas in foil pack on edge of grill while kabobs are cooking.

Remove chicken and vegetables from skewers. Divide evenly among tortillas; fold in half. Serve with sour cream mixture and salsa.

TACO BELL and HOME ORIGINALS are registered trademarks owned and licensed by Taco Bell Corp.

BBQ Chicken *Wrap* Sandwiches

Prep time: 15 minutes   Grilling time: 12 minutes

Makes 4 servings

1   **pound boneless skinless chicken breast halves**
2   **medium green peppers, quartered**
1   **medium onion, sliced**
1   **cup KRAFT Original Barbecue Sauce**
8   **flour tortillas (6 inch) *or* 4 flour tortillas (10 inch), warmed**

Place chicken and vegetables on greased grill over medium coals.

Grill chicken 10 to 12 minutes or until cooked through (160°F) and vegetables 8 to 10 minutes, brushing each frequently with sauce and turning occasionally.

Cool slightly; slice chicken and vegetables into thin strips. Divide filling among tortillas. Fold up sides of tortilla to center, slightly overlapping. Secure with toothpick, if desired. Serve with additional sauce.

Grilled Vegetables

When vegetables are in season, purchase a variety and grill them brushed with KRAFT Italian Dressing. Just like the peppers and onions in the recipe above, eggplant, zucchini, yellow summer squash, asparagus and mushrooms are also delicious hot off the grill.

Cheesy Chicken Fajitas

Prep time: 10 minutes   Grilling time: 15 minutes

Makes 6 servings

3   boneless skinless chicken breast halves (about ¾ pound)
1   clove garlic, halved
1   medium green *or* red pepper, quartered
½   cup red onion, sliced ¼ inch thick
1½ cups KRAFT Mexican Style Shredded Cheese
6   flour tortillas (6 inch), warmed
    TACO BELL HOME ORIGINALS Thick 'N Chunky Salsa

Rub both sides of chicken with garlic clove. Place chicken, green pepper and onion slices on greased grill over medium coals.

Grill 12 to 15 minutes or until cooked through (160°F), turning once. Cool slightly; cut chicken and green pepper into thin strips.

Place chicken mixture and ¼ cup cheese on center of each tortilla; fold. Serve with salsa.

TACO BELL and HOME ORIGINALS are registered trademarks owned and licensed by Taco Bell Corp.

Outdoor Dinners

Make the most of the sunny season by preparing and eating meals in your backyard. Forget fussy foods and choose meals that are as easy to transport as they are to prepare, such as meal-size salads, hearty sandwiches and easy-to-assemble items like fajitas, tacos and wraps. Call on unbreakable or disposable dinnerware and glasses.

Zesty Grilled Turkey Burgers

Prep time: 10 minutes   Grilling time: 18 minutes

Makes 4

1   package (16 ounces) **LOUIS RICH** Frozen
      Ground Turkey, thawed
1   envelope **GOOD SEASONS** Garlic & Herb
      Salad Dressing Mix
4   Kaiser rolls, split, toasted
4   to 8 **CLAUSSEN** Burger Slices

Mix turkey and salad dressing mix. Shape into 4 patties.

Place patties on grill over medium coals. Grill 7 to 9 minutes on each side or until cooked through (165°F).

Fill rolls with patties and pickle slices.

Lemon Dill Fish

Prep time: 10 minutes plus marinating   Grilling or Broiling time: 12 minutes

Makes 6 to 8 servings

1	envelope GOOD SEASONS Zesty Italian *or* Italian Salad Dressing Mix
¼	cup oil
¼	cup chopped fresh parsley
2	tablespoons lemon juice
1	teaspoon dill weed
2	pounds salmon fillets *or* swordfish steaks

Mix salad dressing mix, oil, parsley, juice and dill in cruet or small bowl as directed on envelope.

Rub over fish in large glass baking dish; cover. Refrigerate 1 hour to marinate. Drain, discarding marinade.

Place fish on greased grill over medium coals or on rack of broiler pan 2 to 4 inches from heat. Grill or broil 4 to 6 minutes on each side or until fish flakes easily with fork.

Lemon Juice Savvy

Freshly squeezed lemon juice gives a tantalizing citrus flavor to all types of dishes. To get the most juice, purchase a lemon that is heavy for its size. Before squeezing, leave the lemon at room temperature for 30 minutes. Then roll it under the palm of your hand a few times so more juice will flow. A medium lemon will yield about 3 tablespoons juice.

SEVEN SEAS® Simply *Marinade*

Prep time: 5 minutes plus marinating   Grilling or Broiling time: 18 minutes

Makes 4 to 6 servings

1   cup SEVEN SEAS VIVA Italian Dressing, divided
1½   pounds fish and vegetables

Pour ¾ cup of the dressing over fish and vegetables in glass baking dish; cover.

Refrigerate 30 minutes to 1 hour to marinate. Drain, discarding marinade.

Place fish and vegetables on greased grill over medium coals or on rack of broiler pan 4 to 6 inches from heat. Grill or broil to desired doneness, turning and brushing with remaining ¼ cup dressing. Garnish with fresh tarragon and dill flower.

Grilled Italian *Shrimp*

Prep time: 10 minutes   Grilling time: 8 minutes

Makes 12 servings

1   envelope **GOOD SEASONS Italian Salad Dressing Mix**

⅓   cup olive oil

¼   cup balsamic vinegar

1   pound medium shrimp, cleaned

½   pound hard salami, cut into ¼-inch cubes

½   pound fresh mozzarella cheese, thinly sliced

2   tablespoons chopped fresh basil

Mix salad dressing mix, oil and vinegar in cruet or small bowl as directed on envelope.

Thread shrimp and salami onto four skewers.

Place kabobs on greased grill over medium coals. Grill 6 to 8 minutes or until shrimp turn pink, turning once. Remove from skewers.

Arrange cheese slices on platter; top with shrimp and salami. Drizzle with dressing mixture; sprinkle with basil. Serve with bread, if desired.

Salad Dressing to the Rescue

Mix up your favorite GOOD SEASONS Salad Dressing Mix and keep some on hand to add a flavor boost to all types of foods. (It will store in the refrigerator for up to 4 weeks.) Use it as a dip for crusty bread or vegetables. Brush some on chicken, seafood or meats before grilling or roasting. Sauté vegetables or meats in the dressing for extra zing.

Margarita Shrimp and Vegetable Kabobs

Prep time: 20 minutes plus marinating   Grilling time: 15 minutes

Makes 4 servings

¼ cup *each* tequila and lime juice
1 envelope GOOD SEASONS Italian *or*
    Zesty Italian Salad Dressing Mix
½ cup oil
1 pound medium shrimp, cleaned
    Assorted cut-up fresh vegetables (red
    peppers, onions, zucchini, yellow
    summer squash, mushrooms)

Mix tequila, juice, salad dressing mix and oil in cruet or small bowl as directed on envelope. Pour over shrimp and vegetables in large zipper-style plastic bag; seal bag. Refrigerate 1 hour to marinate. Drain, discarding marinade.

Arrange shrimp and vegetables on skewers.

Place kabobs on greased grill over medium coals. Grill 10 to 15 minutes or until shrimp turn pink and vegetables are tender-crisp, turning once. Serve with rice.

Tails Up

For an extra-special presentation, leave the tails on the shrimp for Margarita Shrimp and Vegetable Kabobs.

Simple Summer Marinades

GOOD SEASONS Italian Salad Dressing Mix makes a flavorful marinade, whether it's prepared as directed or made with one of the four variations listed below.

Pour dressing over meat or vegetables and marinate according to the chart below. For food safety reasons, do not marinate meat and vegetables together and discard marinade after use.

Meat or Vegetable	Amount of Time to Marinate
1 pound beef	4 hours to overnight
1½ pounds chicken	1 hour to overnight
1 pound fish	30 minutes to 1 hour
1½ pounds vegetables	30 minutes to 1 hour

Citrus Marinade: Mix 1 envelope GOOD SEASONS Italian Salad Dressing Mix, ⅓ cup oil and ⅓ cup orange juice.

Italian Marinade: Mix 1 envelope GOOD SEASONS Italian Salad Dressing Mix, ⅓ cup oil, ⅓ cup dry white wine and 2 tablespoons lemon juice.

Teriyaki Marinade: Mix 1 envelope GOOD SEASONS Italian Salad Dressing Mix, ¼ cup cider vinegar, ¼ cup oil, ¼ cup soy sauce and 2 tablespoons honey.

Margarita Marinade: Mix 1 envelope GOOD SEASONS Italian Salad Dressing Mix, ½ cup oil and ¼ cup *each* lime juice and tequila.

Simple Salad Meal

For a light summer meal, serve your marinated grilled chicken, fish or meat over mixed greens that are tossed with additional prepared GOOD SEASONS Salad Dressing.

BBQ sauce *sensations*

To spice up chicken, burgers, chops, steaks or ribs, simply add one of these flavorful stir-ins to 1 cup KRAFT Original Barbecue Sauce.

Southern
½ teaspoon hot pepper sauce and ¼ teaspoon garlic powder

Curry
2 teaspoons curry powder

Mexican
1 ½ teaspoons chili powder and ¼ teaspoon garlic powder

Sweet Onion
½ cup firmly packed brown sugar, 2 tablespoons KRAFT Pure Prepared Mustard and 1 tablespoon dried minced onion

Southwestern Chile
1 can (4 ounces) chopped green chiles, drained

Orange
2 tablespoons thawed orange juice concentrate and ¼ teaspoon crushed red pepper

Oriental
2 tablespoons soy sauce, ½ teaspoon minced peeled gingerroot and ¼ teaspoon garlic powder

Cranberry
½ cup chopped dried cranberries

Sweet Pineapple
1 can (8¼ ounces) crushed pineapple, drained

VELVEETA® Broccoli Dip
(recipe, page 72), Tropical
Fruit Punch (recipe, page 84)
and CRACKER BARREL®
Snacks (recipe, page 72)

ON-THE-DECK SNACKS AND SIPPERS

The meat is on the grill but everyone is hungry now. Here's an inviting assortment of simple meal starters to tide everyone over until the grilling is finished. The kids will love to munch on Quick Microwave Nachos and Tropical Fruit Punch. For the adults? Serve Easy Bruschetta and Cinnamon Caramel Iced Coffee. The compliments will come pouring in.

VELVEETA® *Broccoli* Dip

(Photo on pages 70–71.)

Prep time: 5 minutes   Microwaving time: 6 minutes

Makes 2¾ cups

1	**package (10 ounces) frozen chopped broccoli**
1	**pound (16 ounces) VELVEETA Pasteurized Prepared Cheese Product, cut up**
½	**teaspoon garlic powder**

Microwave broccoli in covered 2-quart microwavable casserole on HIGH 3 minutes or until thawed; drain.

Add prepared cheese product and garlic powder. Microwave 2 to 3 minutes or until prepared cheese product is melted, stirring after 2 minutes.

Serve hot with chips and assorted cut-up vegetables.

CRACKER BARREL® *Snacks*

What could be easier, or more appealing, than serving CRACKER BARREL Extra Sharp Cheddar Cheese with whole wheat crackers and fruit? No fruit on hand? Substitute jelly, sliced ripe olives or roasted sweet red peppers.

Quick Microwave Nachos

Prep time: 10 minutes   Microwaving time: 3 minutes

Tortilla chips
**KRAFT Four Cheese Mexican Style
  Shredded Cheese**
Sliced pitted ripe olives
Chopped green peppers
Chopped tomato

Arrange chips on microwavable plate. Top with remaining ingredients.

Microwave on HIGH 2 to 3 minutes or until cheese is melted.

Refreshing Cucumber,
Dill 'n Cheddar
Snacks

Fruit and Cheese Bites

74

Refreshing Cucumber, Dill 'n Cheddar Snacks

Prep time: 10 minutes

Makes 20

20 crackers
1 package (10 ounces) CRACKER BARREL
Extra Sharp Natural Cheddar Cheese,
thinly sliced
Cucumber slices, cut in half
Fresh dill

Top each cracker with cheese slice, cucumber and dill.

Fruit and Cheese *Bites*

Prep time: 10 minutes

Makes 20

20 table wafer crackers *or* any cracker
1 package (10 ounces) CRACKER BARREL
Extra Sharp Natural Cheddar Cheese,
thinly sliced
Strawberry halves *or* kiwi slices, cut in
half
¼ cup orange marmalade

Top each cracker with cheese slice, fruit and marmalade. Garnish with fresh mint leaves or sprigs of fresh dill.

Easy Bruschetta

Prep time: 15 minutes   Broiling time: 6 minutes

Makes about 3 dozen

1   **loaf French bread *or* baguette, cut into ½-inch-thick slices**
1   **cup KRAFT Italian Dressing**
½   **cup KRAFT 100% Grated Parmesan Cheese**
2   **large tomatoes, chopped**
2   **green onions, chopped**

Place bread slices on cookie sheet. Broil 2 minutes on each side or until golden brown.

Mix dressing and cheese. Reserve ¼ cup dressing mixture. Spread 1 side of toasted bread with remaining dressing mixture. Broil 1 to 2 minutes or until golden brown.

Toss tomatoes and onions with reserved ¼ cup dressing mixture. Top bread slices with tomato mixture.

Cheezy Beer Dip

Prep time: 5 minutes   Microwaving time: 2 minutes

Makes 2 cups

1   **jar (15 ounces) CHEEZ WHIZ Cheese Dip**

⅓   **cup beer**

Microwave cheese dip as directed on label.

Mix cheese dip and beer in bowl, stirring until mixture becomes smooth. Garnish with sliced green onion. Serve with pretzels, breadsticks or green onions.

Italian *Spinach* Dip

Prep time: 10 minutes plus refrigerating

Makes 3 cups

1   **cup KRAFT Mayo Real Mayonnaise**
1   **cup BREAKSTONE'S *or* KNUDSEN Sour Cream**
1   **envelope GOOD SEASONS Italian Salad Dressing Mix**
1   **package (10 ounces) frozen chopped spinach, thawed, well drained**
½   **cup chopped red pepper (optional)**

Mix mayo, sour cream and salad dressing mix until well blended. Add spinach and red pepper; mix well. Refrigerate.

Serve in hollowed-out red cabbage with assorted fresh vegetables.

Serving Dips and Spreads

For a splash of color, serve dips and spreads in edible containers—hollowed-out round bread loaves, bell peppers, zucchini and small red or green cabbages are great to make into "bowls." After filling with dip, set the "bowl" on a serving plate and surround it with an assortment of crackers, chips and/or bite-size fresh veggies.

PHILADELPHIA® Creamy *Salsa Dip*

Prep time: 10 minutes plus refrigerating

Makes 2 cups

1   **package (8 ounces) PHILADELPHIA Cream
    Cheese, softened**
1   **cup TACO BELL HOME ORIGINALS Salsa,
    any variety**

Mix cream cheese and salsa until well blended. Refrigerate. Garnish with zucchini and carrot curl. Serve with crackers, tortilla chips or assorted cut-up vegetables.

TACO BELL and HOME ORIGINALS are registered trademarks owned and licensed by Taco Bell Corp.

Antipasto

Prep time: 15 minutes plus marinating

Makes 8 to 10 servings

1   bottle (8 ounces) SEVEN SEAS VIVA Italian Dressing

1   package (3 ounces) OSCAR MAYER Pepperoni Slices

1   can (14 ounces) artichoke hearts, drained, quartered

1   cup halved cherry tomatoes

1   cup pitted ripe olives

10 pepperoncini

4   ounces KRAFT Low-Moisture Part-Skim Mozzarella Cheese, cut into ¼-inch sticks

Pour dressing over pepperoni, artichoke hearts, tomatoes, olives and pepperoncini; cover. Refrigerate overnight to marinate. Drain, reserving dressing.

Toss pepperoni, vegetables and cheese with reserved dressing. Spoon onto serving platter.

Nacho Platter Olé

Prep time: 10 minutes   Microwaving time: 10 minutes

Makes 6 to 8 servings

1   can (16 ounces) TACO BELL
      HOME ORIGINALS Refried Beans
1   package (8 to 11 ounces) tortilla chips
1   can (15 ounces) chili
1   jar (15 ounces) CHEEZ WHIZ Cheese Dip

Spread beans onto center of large serving platter.

Arrange chips around beans. Heat chili as directed on label; pour over beans.

Microwave cheese dip as directed on label; pour over chili and chips. Garnish with shredded lettuce and chopped red pepper. Serve immediately.

TACO BELL and HOME ORIGINALS are registered trademarks owned and licensed by Taco Bell Corp.

Company-Special Snack

Serve Nacho Platter Olé when friends drop by for a visit. For a footed platter, turn a saucer or small bowl upside down and place the platter of nachos on top. Then, set the table with bowls of sour cream, salsa, chopped green onions, guacamole and tomatoes so guests can add more toppings to their nachos.

Aloha Punch

Prep time: 5 minutes plus refrigerating

Makes 10 servings

1   tub CRYSTAL LIGHT TROPICAL PASSIONS
     Low Calorie Soft Drink Mix, any
     flavor
4   cups (1 quart) chilled pineapple juice
2   cups cold water
1   bottle (1 liter) chilled club soda
     Ice cubes

Place drink mix in large glass or plastic pitcher. Add pineapple juice and water; stir to dissolve. Refrigerate.

Add club soda and ice just before serving. Garnish with maraschino cherries and orange and pineapple slices arranged on bamboo skewers.

Tropical *Fruit Punch*

(Photo on pages 70–71.)

Prep time: 10 minutes plus refrigerating

Makes 10 servings

½   cup KOOL-AID Tropical Punch *or*
     Lemonade Flavor Sugar-Sweetened
     Soft Drink Mix
6   cups cold water and ice cubes
2   cups chilled mango nectar *or* apricot
     nectar
1   cup chilled orange juice

Place drink mix in large (12-cup) plastic or glass pitcher or punch bowl. Add water and ice cubes; stir to dissolve.

Stir in mango nectar and orange juice. Refrigerate until ready to serve.

Aloha Punch
(recipe, opposite)

Island Swizzle (front) and
Lemonade Float (back)
(recipes, opposite)

Lemonade Floats

Prep time: 5 minutes

Makes 4 servings

COUNTRY TIME Lemonade Flavor Drink Mix *or* **COUNTRY TIME LEM'N BERRY SIPPERS Drink Mix** *or* **COUNTRY TIME Lemonade Iced Tea, any flavor**
4 **cups cold water**
Assorted flavors of sorbet *or* **sherbet**

Measure drink mix into cap just to 1-quart line. Place drink mix in large plastic or glass pitcher. Add cold water; stir to dissolve.

Place 1 scoop sorbet in each tall serving glass. Pour lemonade over sorbet. Stir and serve.

Island *Swizzle*

Prep time: 5 minutes

Makes 6 servings

1 **tub CRYSTAL LIGHT TROPICAL PASSIONS Strawberry Kiwi** *or* **Strawberry Orange Banana Flavor Low Calorie Soft Drink Mix**
1½ **cups cold water**
½ **cup chilled orange juice**
1 **tablespoon lime juice**
4 **cups crushed ice**

Place drink mix, water, orange juice and lime juice in blender container; cover. Blend on high speed until drink mix is dissolved. Add ice; blend until smooth.

Berry Cooler
(recipe, opposite)

Berry *Cooler*

Prep time: 5 minutes plus refrigerating

Makes 9 servings

1   tub CRYSTAL LIGHT Raspberry Ice *or* CRYSTAL LIGHT TROPICAL PASSIONS Strawberry Kiwi Flavor Low Calorie Soft Drink Mix
4   cups cold water, divided
1   pint strawberries, hulled
3   tablespoons lime juice
1   bottle (1 liter) chilled club soda
    Ice cubes

Place drink mix, 1 cup of the water and strawberries in blender container; cover. Blend on high speed until smooth. Pour into large plastic or glass pitcher. Stir in remaining 3 cups water and lime juice. Refrigerate until ready to serve.

Stir in club soda just before serving. Serve over ice.

Cinnamon *Caramel* Iced Coffee

Prep time: 10 minutes plus refrigerating

Makes 6 servings

6   tablespoons MAXWELL HOUSE *or* YUBAN Coffee, any variety
½   teaspoon ground cinnamon
½   cup caramel dessert topping
4½ cups cold water
     Ice cubes

Place coffee in filter in brew basket of coffee maker; sprinkle with cinnamon. Place topping in empty pot of coffee maker. Prepare coffee with cold water. When brewing is complete, stir until well mixed. Refrigerate until ready to serve.

Pour coffee over ice cubes in tall glasses. Serve with milk and sugar, if desired. Top each serving with thawed COOL WHIP Whipped Topping and chopped chocolate-covered toffee, if desired.

Clockwise from back left:
Greek Vegetable Salad
(recipe, page 92),
Antipasto Pasta Salad
(recipe, page 108) and
Sweet and Spicy Pickled
Veggies (recipe, page 93)

PERFECT PARTNERS

Who wants to mess with the oven during the dog days of summer? Turn to the recipes in this chapter for easy-on-the-cook, but definitely delicious, partners for your grilled meat, poultry or fish. Most of these sides require no more preparation than tossing, stirring or wrapping in foil to grill alongside the main course. These serve-alongs may get second billing but they're guaranteed to be first-rate.

Greek Vegetable Salad

(Photo on pages 90–91.)

Prep time: 10 minutes plus refrigerating

Makes 4 side-dish servings

1 **cucumber, seeded, diced**	**Toss** vegetables in large bowl.
1 **large tomato, seeded, diced**	
1 **green pepper, diced**	**Add** dressing; toss lightly. Sprinkle with
½ **cup sliced radishes**	cheese. Refrigerate at least 30 minutes.
½ **small red onion, thinly sliced**	
½ **cup KRAFT Special Collection Greek Vinaigrette Dressing**	
ATHENOS Crumbled Feta Cheese (optional)	

How to Seed Vegetables

Seeding the vegetables keeps the dressing from becoming too watery. To seed tomatoes, slice in half horizontally; then squeeze gently to remove seeds. To seed cucumbers, cut in half lengthwise; use a teaspoon to scoop out the seeds.

Sweet and *Spicy Pickled* Veggies

(Photo on pages 90–91.)

Prep time: 10 minutes plus marinating

Makes 4 cups

1   cup CLAUSSEN Bread 'N Butter Pickle Chips, drained, reserving ½ cup liquid

10   cherry tomatoes, halved, or 1 medium tomato, cut into chunks

1   large carrot, sliced diagonally

½   small onion, cut into strips

¼   cup pickled jalapeño pepper slices, drained, reserving 2 tablespoons liquid

Mix all ingredients and reserved pickle and jalapeño liquids in covered container or zipper-style plastic bag.

Refrigerate 2 hours or overnight to marinate.

Easy Greek Salad

Prep time: 10 minutes

Makes 4 side-dish servings

10 **cups torn romaine lettuce**
 3 **plum tomatoes, cut into wedges**
 ½ **medium cucumber, cut in half lengthwise, sliced**
 ¾ **cup prepared GOOD SEASONS Ripe Olive Italian Dressing (recipe, page 104)**
     ATHENOS Feta Cheese, crumbled

Toss lettuce, tomatoes and cucumber in large bowl. Drizzle with dressing. Sprinkle with cheese.

Beat-the-Heat Sides

When you plan a grilled main course, there's no need to turn on the oven for a single side dish. Here are some mix-and-serve side dishes to complete your meal.

- Toss together canned green beans, roasted red peppers and KRAFT Italian Dressing.

- Arrange a sampling of fresh veggies—cherry tomatoes, sliced zucchini, broccoli flowerets, carrot sticks and green or red pepper strips. Set out some KRAFT Dip for before-dinner nibbling or pass with veggies at the table.

- Arrange a plate of cut-up fresh fruit and cheese cubes. Try KRAFT Cheddar, Swiss and Monterey Jack Cheese with sliced nectarines, sweet cherries and grapes. Brush nectarines with lemon juice to keep them looking fresh.

- Toss mixed salad greens with sliced peaches or strawberries and toasted chopped nuts. Drizzle with KRAFT Balsamic or Strawberry Vinaigrette Dressing.

Grilled *Tri-Colored* Pepper & Mushroom Salad

Prep time: 10 minutes   Grilling time: 12 minutes

Makes 6 side-dish servings

1   *each* **green, red and yellow pepper**
8   **ounces portobello mushroom caps**
¾   **cup KRAFT LIGHT DONE RIGHT Red Wine Vinaigrette Dressing, divided**

Cut peppers lengthwise into quarters. Toss peppers and mushrooms with ½ cup of the dressing.

Place vegetables on grill over medium coals. Grill 10 to 12 minutes or until tender, turning and brushing occasionally with dressing.

Slice mushrooms. Toss mushrooms, peppers and remaining ¼ cup dressing.

Creamy Garden Vegetable Salad

Prep time: 10 minutes

Makes 8 side-dish servings

4 cups *each* **broccoli flowerets and cauliflowerets**

1 pint **cherry tomatoes, halved**

1 cup **KRAFT LIGHT DONE RIGHT Ranch Dressing**

¼ cup **KRAFT 100% Grated Parmesan Cheese**

Toss all ingredients.

Italian Bacon Spinach Salad

Prep time: 10 minutes   Microwaving time: 30 seconds

Makes 8 side-dish servings

8   slices **OSCAR MAYER Ready-To-Serve Bacon, cut into ½-inch pieces, or OSCAR MAYER Center Cut Bacon, cut into ¼-inch pieces, cooked, drained**
¼   cup **KRAFT House Italian Dressing**
6   cups **torn spinach**
1   small **tomato, seeded, chopped**
¼   cup **KRAFT Mozzarella & Parmesan Italian Style Shredded Cheese**
     Fresh ground pepper (optional)

Place bacon and dressing in small microwavable bowl. Microwave on HIGH 30 seconds or until warm.

Toss dressing with spinach and tomato in large bowl.

Sprinkle with cheese. Season to taste with pepper; toss lightly. Serve immediately.

Summertime Spinach Salad

Prep time: 15 minutes

Makes 8 to 10 side-dish servings

1   **package (10 ounces) spinach leaves**
2   **cups sugar snap peas *or* pea pods**
2   **cups sliced strawberries**
½   **medium red onion, cut into thin wedges**
½   **cup sliced almonds, toasted**
¾   **cup KRAFT Classic Italian Vinaigrette**
     Dressing

Toss all ingredients.

Farmers' Market Toss

Prep time: 15 minutes plus refrigerating

Makes 6 side-dish servings

1   **cup BREAKSTONE'S *or* KNUDSEN Sour Cream**

1   **envelope GOOD SEASONS Italian Salad Dressing Mix**

4   **cups torn romaine *or* iceberg lettuce**

3   **cups assorted sliced *or* chopped vegetables**

1   **can (14 ounces) artichoke hearts, drained, cut up**

Mix sour cream and salad dressing mix. Refrigerate.

Toss lettuce, vegetables and artichokes in large bowl. Top with desired amount of sour cream mixture; toss until evenly coated. Store any remaining sour cream mixture in refrigerator.

Gourmet Grilled Vegetable Salad

Prep time: 10 minutes   Grilling time: 30 minutes

Makes 6 side-dish servings

¼   **cup cider vinegar**
2   **tablespoons water**
1   **envelope GOOD SEASONS Gourmet Parmesan Italian *or* Italian Salad Dressing Mix**
⅓   **cup olive oil**
1   **pound small red potatoes, cut into quarters**
1   ***each* zucchini and yellow squash, halved lengthwise, cut into ½-inch chunks**
1   **cup slivered red onion**

Mix vinegar, water, salad dressing mix and oil in cruet or small bowl as directed on envelope. Toss with vegetables.

Spoon mixture evenly onto double layer of heavy-duty foil; close foil to form tightly sealed pouch.

Place pouch on greased grill over medium coals. Grill 30 minutes, turning and shaking pouch halfway through grilling time. Garnish with fresh rosemary.

Cook on the Range

Prepare dressing as directed for Gourmet Grilled Vegetable Salad; set aside. Boil potatoes in 6 quarts water for 10 minutes. Add zucchini, squash and onion; boil 5 minutes or until vegetables are tender. Drain; toss vegetables with dressing. Serve immediately.

cooking without *recipes*

*Start with 1 envelope GOOD SEASONS Italian
Salad Dressing Mix and try these flavorful variations.*

Zesty Lemon:
Capture the taste of
summer: Use ¼ cup
fresh squeezed lemon
juice instead of vinegar
and prepare dressing
as directed.

Balsamic Vinaigrette:
Capture a classic Italian
taste: Use balsamic vinegar
instead of regular vinegar
and prepare dressing as
directed.

Parmesan Italian:
Indulge the cheese
lovers in your life:
Prepare dressing as
directed and add
2 tablespoons KRAFT
100% Grated
Parmesan
Cheese.

Robust Italian: Liven up
your salads with a robust
flavor: Prepare dressing as
directed and add 2 teaspoons
Worcestershire sauce.

Ripe Olive Italian: Conjure
up the sun-drenched warmth of
the Mediterranean: Prepare
dressing as directed and add
2 tablespoons diced ripe olives.

Garden *Fresh* Potato Salad

Prep time: 20 minutes plus refrigerating

Makes 6 side-dish servings

4 cups cubed cooked potatoes
¾ cup KRAFT Savory Mayo Roasted Onion
    Mayonnaise Dressing *or* MIRACLE WHIP
    Zesty Onion Dressing
½ cup *each* shredded carrot and chopped
    cucumber

Mix potatoes, mayo, carrot and cucumber in large bowl. Refrigerate.

Roasted Garlic Potato Salad

Prepare Garden Fresh Potato Salad as directed, substituting KRAFT Savory Mayo Roasted Garlic Mayonnaise Dressing *or* MIRACLE WHIP Roasted Garlic Dressing for Roasted Onion Mayonnaise Dressing.

Hot German Potato Salad

Prep time: 15 minutes   Grilling time: 30 minutes

Makes 6 side-dish servings

½   cup cider vinegar
1   envelope GOOD SEASONS Gourmet
    Caesar Salad Dressing Mix
¼   cup oil
6   medium potatoes, peeled, sliced
1   medium onion, chopped
8   slices bacon, cut into 1-inch pieces,
    cooked, crumbled

Mix vinegar, salad dressing mix and oil in cruet or small bowl as directed on envelope. Toss with vegetables and cooked bacon.

Spoon mixture evenly onto double layer of heavy-duty foil; close foil to form tightly sealed pouch.

Place pouch on greased grill over medium coals. Grill 30 minutes, turning and shaking pouch halfway through grilling time.

Dinner from the Grill

With foil-packet recipes such as Hot German Potato Salad, above, cooking a meal on the grill is easy. Simply grill the packet alongside steaks, chops, burgers, chicken pieces or fish. If the meat or fish takes longer to cook than the packet, start the meat first, then add the foil pouch. After grilling, open the foil slowly, being careful to allow steam to escape away from you.

Italian Pasta Salad

Prep time: 15 minutes plus refrigerating

Makes 8 side-dish servings

3 cups (8 ounces) rotini pasta, cooked, drained

2 cups broccoli flowerets

1 bottle (8 ounces) KRAFT House Italian Dressing

1 cup KRAFT 100% Grated Parmesan Cheese

½ cup *each* chopped red pepper, pitted ripe olives and slivered red onion

Toss all ingredients. Refrigerate.

Antipasto Pasta Salad

(Photo on pages 90–91.)

Prep time: 15 minutes

Makes 6 side-dish servings

1 **package (9.15 ounces) KRAFT 97% Fat Free Italian Pasta Salad**	**Prepare** Pasta Salad as directed on package.
½ **cup cubed KRAFT Low-Moisture Part-Skim Mozzarella Cheese**	**Stir** in remaining ingredients. Serve immediately or refrigerate.
6 **slices OSCAR MAYER Hard Salami, cut into strips,** *or* ¼ **cup DI GIORNO Pepperoni, cut into quarters**	
¼ **cup thinly sliced red onion**	

Mediterranean Rice Salad

Prep time: 20 minutes plus refrigerating

Makes 8 side-dish servings

3 **cups MINUTE Brown Rice, cooked**	**Mix** all ingredients except dressing in large bowl.
1½ **cups quartered cucumber slices**	**Add** dressing; toss to coat. Refrigerate.
1 **cup chopped seeded tomato**	
1 **can (4½ ounces) sliced pitted ripe olives, drained**	
½ **cup chopped onion**	
¼ **cup chopped fresh parsley**	
¾ **cup SEVEN SEAS VIVA Italian Dressing**	

Mediterranean
Rice Salad
(recipe, opposite)

Sparkling Mandarin Orange Pineapple Mold

Prep time: 20 minutes   Refrigerating time: 4¾ hours

Makes 10 side-dish servings

1½   **cups boiling water**
 2   **packages (4-serving size *each*) JELL-O Brand Sparkling Mandarin Orange Flavor Gelatin**
 2   **cups chilled club soda *or* seltzer**
 1   **can (11 ounces) mandarin orange segments, drained**
 1   **can (8 ounces) pineapple chunks, drained**

Stir boiling water into gelatin in large bowl at least 2 minutes until completely dissolved. Refrigerate 15 minutes. Gently stir in chilled club soda. Refrigerate about 30 minutes or until slightly thickened (consistency of unbeaten egg whites). Gently stir for 15 seconds.

Stir in orange segments and pineapple gently. Spoon into 6-cup mold.

Refrigerate 4 hours or until firm. Unmold. Garnish as desired. Store leftover gelatin mold in refrigerator.

Summer Fruit Basket

Prep time: 20 minutes   Refrigerating time: 5½ hours

Makes 12 side-dish servings

2 **cups boiling water**
1 **package (8-serving size) *or* 2 packages (4-serving size *each*) JELL-O Brand Strawberry Flavor Gelatin *or* any red fruit flavor**
1½ **cups chilled ginger ale *or* water**
1 **cup sliced strawberries**
1 **cup green grape halves**
1 **cup cantaloupe cubes**

Stir boiling water into gelatin in large bowl at least 2 minutes until completely dissolved. Stir in chilled ginger ale. Refrigerate about 1½ hours or until thickened (spoon drawn through leaves definite impression).

Stir in fruit. Pour into 6-cup mold.

Refrigerate 4 hours or until firm. Unmold. Garnish as desired. Store leftover gelatin mold in refrigerator.

How to Unmold a Gelatin Salad

To remove a gelatin salad from a mold, dip the mold in warm water about 15 seconds. With moist fingers, gently pull the gelatin from around edges. Place a moistened serving plate on top of mold. Invert the mold and plate. Holding the mold and plate together, shake slightly to loosen. Gently remove the mold and center the gelatin on the plate.

Strawberry and Melon *Salad*

Prep time: 20 minutes

Makes 12 side-dish servings

¼ **cup orange juice**
1 **envelope GOOD SEASONS Italian Salad**
   Dressing Mix
½ **cup oil**
2 **tablespoons water**
1 **package (10 ounces) salad greens**
3 **cups melon balls** *or* **chunks**
1 **cup sliced strawberries**
3 **tablespoons sunflower seeds**

Pour juice into cruet or medium bowl. Add salad dressing mix, oil and water. Shake vigorously or mix until well blended.

Toss greens, melon, strawberries and dressing in large bowl. Sprinkle with sunflower seeds.

Grilled Italian *Focaccia*

Prep time: 10 minutes plus rising   Grilling time: 8 minutes

Makes 2 bread rounds or 16 servings

1 **package (16 ounces) hot roll mix**
1 **envelope GOOD SEASONS Italian Salad Dressing Mix**
3 **tablespoons olive oil, divided**
1 **cup DI GIORNO Shredded Parmesan Cheese**
2 **plum tomatoes, sliced**
2 **tablespoons fresh basil leaves**

Mix hot roll mix, yeast packet and salad dressing mix. Add 1¼ cups hot water (120°F to 130°F) and 2 tablespoons of the oil. Stir until soft dough forms and dough pulls away from side of bowl.

Knead dough on lightly floured surface about 5 minutes or until smooth and elastic. Shape dough into 2 (10-inch) rounds. Cover with plastic wrap or towel. Let rise in warm place 15 minutes.

Place dough rounds on greased grill over medium-low coals. Grill 4 minutes; turn. Brush with remaining 1 tablespoon oil. Top with cheese and tomatoes. Grill an additional 4 minutes or until bottom crust is golden brown. Top with basil.

Grilled Bread

Prep time: 5 minutes   Grilling time: 6 minutes

Makes 12 servings

1   **bottle (8 ounces) KRAFT House Italian with Olive Oil Blend Dressing**
1   **loaf French bread, cut into slices**

Spread dressing generously over cut surfaces of bread. Place on grill over medium coals.

Grill 3 minutes on each side or until toasted. Serve with salads or grilled meats.

Spicy Vegetable Couscous

(Photo on page 46.)

Prep time: 15 minutes   Cooking time: 12 minutes plus standing

Makes 6 side-dish servings

1   **can (13¾ ounces) chicken broth**
1   **cup couscous**
2   **tablespoons olive oil**
1   **cup *each* chopped zucchini and red onion**
½   **cup grated carrots**
1   **clove garlic, minced**
1   **can (19 ounces) garbanzo beans (chickpeas), rinsed, drained**
½   **teaspoon *each* ground cumin, curry powder, salt and red pepper flakes**

Bring broth to a boil. Stir in couscous. Remove from heat. Let stand, covered, 5 minutes.

Heat oil in large skillet. Add zucchini, onion, carrots and garlic; cook and stir 5 minutes or until tender.

Add beans, seasonings and couscous; cook and stir until thoroughly heated, about 2 minutes.

Grilled Parmesan Corn

Give corn on the cob a delicious twist by grilling it. Soak unhusked corn in water for 2 hours, then grill it over medium-hot coals for 20 minutes or until tender. Turn corn frequently to prevent burning. Brush the husked corn with softened butter, then roll it in KRAFT 100% Grated Parmesan Cheese. Your family will love it!

Caesar Potatoes

Prep time: 10 minutes   Grilling time: 35 minutes

Makes 4 to 6 servings

1   **envelope GOOD SEASONS Gourmet Caesar *or* Italian Salad Dressing Mix**
¼   **cup *each* cider vinegar and oil**
1½   **pounds red potatoes, cut into chunks**
1   **medium red *or* green pepper, cut into 1-inch pieces**
1   **medium onion, cut into 1-inch pieces**

Prepare salad dressing mix in cruet or small bowl as directed on envelope with vinegar and oil, omitting water.

Toss remaining ingredients with dressing mixture. Spoon evenly onto double layer of heavy-duty foil; close foil to form tightly sealed pouch.

Place pouch on greased grill over medium coals. Grill 30 to 35 minutes or until potatoes are tender, turning and shaking pouch halfway through grilling time.

Great in the Oven, Too!

Prepare Caesar Potatoes as directed except for grilling. Spoon potatoes evenly into 15×10×1-inch baking pan lined with foil. Bake at 400°F for 40 minutes or until potatoes are tender.

Spicy Grilled *Mushrooms*

Prep time: 5 minutes plus marinating   Grilling or Broiling time: 10 minutes

Makes 4 to 6 servings

¼   **cup cider vinegar**
3   **tablespoons soy sauce**
1   **envelope GOOD SEASONS Oriental Sesame Salad Dressing Mix**
½   **cup oil**
1   **to 2 teaspoons hot pepper sauce**
2   **cloves garlic, minced**
1   **pound fresh shiitake *or* button mushrooms, stems removed**

Mix vinegar, soy sauce, salad dressing mix, oil, hot pepper sauce and garlic in cruet or small bowl as directed on envelope. Pour over mushrooms in large bowl. Let stand 30 minutes to marinate. Drain, reserving dressing mixture.

Place mushrooms on greased grill over medium coals or on rack of broiler pan 3 to 5 inches from heat. Grill or broil mushrooms 3 to 5 minutes on each side or until tender and slightly crisp, turning and brushing frequently with reserved dressing mixture.

Clockwise from front: Antipasto
Salad (recipe, page 125), Pesto
Garden Salad (recipe, page 133)
and Tomatoes & Spinach
Vinaigrette (recipe, page 133)

POTLUCK FAVORITES

Sharing a meal with family and friends is one of life's simple pleasures, especially when everyone brings a favorite dish to share. If you're looking for a dynamite dish to tote to a potluck or picnic, take a peek at these people-pleasing choices. All of the recipes, including Creamy Hawaiian Fruit Salad and Triple Chocolate Cake, are designed to be easy to transport and to taste great when you get there.

PHILADELPHIA® 7-Layer *Mexican Dip*

Prep time: 10 minutes plus refrigerating

Makes 6 to 8 servings

1 **package (8 ounces) PHILADELPHIA Cream Cheese, softened**
1 **tablespoon TACO BELL HOME ORIGINALS Taco Seasoning Mix**
1 **cup prepared guacamole**
1 **cup TACO BELL HOME ORIGINALS Thick 'N Chunky Salsa**
1 **cup shredded lettuce**
1 **cup KRAFT Shredded Cheddar Cheese**
½ **cup chopped green onions**
2 **tablespoons sliced pitted ripe olives**

Mix cream cheese and seasoning mix. Spread onto bottom of 9-inch pie plate or quiche dish.

Layer remaining ingredients over cream cheese mixture. Refrigerate.

Serve with tortilla chips.

TACO BELL and HOME ORIGINALS are registered trademarks owned and licensed by Taco Bell Corp.

Double Raspberry Fruit Dip

Prep time: 5 minutes plus refrigerating

Makes 2 cups

½ cup SEVEN SEAS FREE Raspberry
Vinaigrette Fat Free Dressing
½ cup BREYERS Lowfat Raspberry Yogurt
1 cup thawed COOL WHIP FREE Whipped
Topping
Cut-up fresh fruit

Mix dressing, yogurt and whipped topping
until smooth. Refrigerate.

Serve with fruit.

BREYERS is a registered trademark owned and licensed by
Unilever, N.V.

Antipasto *Salad*

(Photo on pages 120–121.)

Prep time: 10 minutes

Makes 6 servings

1   **package (10 ounces) salad greens (about 10 cups)**

1   **can (6 ounces) pitted ripe olives, drained, halved**

1   **cup KRAFT Shredded Low-Moisture Part-Skim Mozzarella Cheese**

10 **pepperoncini peppers**

8   **slices OSCAR MAYER Hard Salami, quartered**

¾ **cup SEVEN SEAS VIVA Italian Dressing**

Toss greens with remaining ingredients.

Easy Antipasto Tray

To create an antipasto tray, prepare Antipasto Salad as directed, except omit salad greens and cube the cheese. Toss olives, cheese, peppers and salami with dressing. Decoratively arrange ingredients on a large platter.

Ranch *Taco* Chicken Salad

Prep time: 15 minutes   Cooking time: 8 minutes

Makes 6 servings

1 **pound boneless skinless chicken breast halves, cut into strips**
1 **cup TACO BELL HOME ORIGINALS Thick 'N Chunky Salsa, divided**
1 **package (16 ounces) salad greens**
1 **cup KRAFT Shredded Cheddar Cheese**
1 **cup KRAFT FREE Ranch Fat Free Dressing *or* KRAFT Ranch Dressing**

Cook and stir chicken in ¼ cup of the salsa in large nonstick skillet on medium-high heat 8 minutes or until chicken is cooked through.

Toss chicken, greens and cheese on serving platter or in large bowl.

Top with remaining ¾ cup salsa and dressing before serving. Garnish with chile pepper.

TACO BELL and HOME ORIGINALS are registered trademarks owned and licensed by Taco Bell Corp.

Tarragon Chicken Salad Pitas

Prep time: 15 minutes plus refrigerating

Makes 6

4 boneless skinless chicken breast halves
(about 1¼ pounds), cooked, cubed

1 cup red grapes

¾ cup MIRACLE WHIP Salad Dressing *or*
KRAFT Mayo Real Mayonnaise

1 teaspoon dried tarragon leaves

6 whole wheat pita breads, halved
Lettuce

Mix all ingredients except pita breads and lettuce. Refrigerate several hours or overnight.

Line pita breads with lettuce; fill with chicken salad.

Italian Subs

Prep time: 10 minutes

Makes 4

4 **French bread rolls, split**
¼ **cup KRAFT Italian Dressing**
1 **package (16 ounces) OSCAR MAYER Combo Pack Meats**
2 **KRAFT Low-Moisture Part-Skim Mozzarella Cheese Slices, cut in half**
Thinly sliced onion
Mild pickled pepper rings

Spread bottom half of each roll with 1 tablespoon of the dressing.

Layer with meat, cheese, onion, pepper rings and top half of roll.

Variation: Prepare Italian Subs as directed, substituting KRAFT Special Collection Balsamic Vinaigrette Dressing for Italian Dressing.

Potluck Tips

- Six desserts, no salad? Avoid the "luck of the draw" by assigning food categories for your potluck.

- Ask people to bring a dish that needs no further heating or chilling, along with serving utensils.

- Assign volunteers to organize grills, picnic tables and tableware. Arrange for decorations and entertainment, if they fit your plans, and for cleanup.

Turkey Parmesan *Casserole*

Prep time: 10 minutes   Baking time: 30 minutes

Makes 4 to 6 servings

8 ounces spaghetti, broken in half, cooked and drained

2 cups chopped cooked turkey

1 can (10¾ ounces) condensed cream of mushroom soup

3 cups frozen broccoli flowerets, thawed

1 cup BREAKSTONE'S *or* KNUDSEN Sour Cream

1 cup KRAFT 100% Grated Parmesan Cheese, divided

Mix all ingredients except ¼ cup of the Parmesan cheese in large bowl.

Spoon into 2-quart casserole. Sprinkle with remaining ¼ cup Parmesan cheese.

Bake at 350°F for 25 to 30 minutes or until thoroughly heated.

Toting Foods Safely

The guideline for safe potluck dishes is easy to remember: Serve hot foods piping hot and cold foods cold. Insulated totes are the tools that make this practice easy. And don't let items linger on the table for more than an hour. Refrigerate them immediately or discard.

Italian Garden Salad

Prep time: 10 minutes

Makes 6 side-dish servings

1   **package (10 ounces) mixed Italian greens (about 10 cups)**
1   *each* **small zucchini and small red pepper, sliced**
1   **can (6 ounces) pitted ripe olives, drained**
½   **cup red onion slices**
¾   **cup KRAFT Special Collection Sun Dried Tomato Dressing**

Toss greens with remaining ingredients.

Grilled Chicken Italian Salad

Prepare Italian Garden Salad as directed, except marinate 2 boneless skinless chicken breast halves in ½ cup KRAFT Special Collection Sun Dried Tomato Dressing 30 minutes to 2 hours. Drain. Place chicken on greased grill over medium coals. Grill 12 to 15 minutes or until cooked through (160°F), turning once. Cool slightly; slice chicken. Toss with salad. Makes 4 servings.

Tomatoes & Spinach *Vinaigrette*

(Photo on pages 120–121.)

Prep time: 10 minutes

Makes 6 side-dish servings

2 large tomatoes, sliced
2 cups spinach *or* fresh basil leaves
½ cup KRAFT Classic Italian Vinaigrette Dressing
1 cup KRAFT Shredded Low-Moisture Part-Skim Mozzarella Cheese

Arrange tomatoes and spinach alternately overlapping on platter. Drizzle with dressing.

Sprinkle with cheese.

Pesto Garden Salad

(Photo on pages 120–121.)

Prep time: 10 minutes

Makes 6 to 8 side-dish servings

2 large tomatoes, cut into wedges
½ medium red onion, cut into slivers
½ large cucumber, cut lengthwise, sliced
1 bottle (8 ounces) KRAFT Special Collection Italian Pesto Dressing
2 cups croutons

Mix all ingredients except croutons in large bowl. Toss to mix well.

Stir in croutons just before serving.

Creamy *Hawaiian* Fruit Salad

Prep time: 10 minutes plus refrigerating

Makes 6 side-dish servings

2 cups red grapes

1 cup orange sections

1 banana, sliced

1 can (8 ounces) pineapple chunks, drained

1 cup miniature marshmallows

1 cup BREAKSTONE'S *or* KNUDSEN Sour Cream

Toasted BAKER'S ANGEL FLAKE Coconut (optional)

Mix all ingredients except coconut. Refrigerate several hours or overnight.

Sprinkle with coconut just before serving.

salad *ideas*

Salads are a cool, crisp answer to summertime eating. These fixer-uppers make welcome additions to potluck gatherings.

Hearty Garden Salad

Toss chopped **OSCAR MAYER** Ham & Turkey **VARIETY-PAK** meats, sliced radishes and carrots, chopped green pepper and tomato and torn iceberg lettuce with **KRAFT** Italian Tomato & Herb Dressing.

Greens Mix-Up

Combine various greens, such as oakleaf lettuce, arugula and mesclun (a mix of young, small salad greens), to add color, texture and flavor to salads.

Italian Pasta Spinach Salad

Toss cooked tri-color rotini pasta, quartered marinated artichoke hearts, sliced roasted red peppers, sliced pitted ripe olives and spinach leaves with **KRAFT** House Italian Dressing.

Main Dish Salads

Garden salads turn into delicious entrées with the simple addition of a little protein. Try adding leftover grilled chicken or steak, strips or cubes of **OSCAR MAYER** Ham or **KRAFT** Cheese, canned tuna or hard-boiled eggs.

Chicken Caesar Salad

Toss sliced cooked chicken breast halves, torn romaine lettuce and croutons with **KRAFT** Classic Caesar Dressing. Sprinkle with **KRAFT** 100% Shredded Parmesan Cheese.

Toppings from the Pantry

Add new personality to a tossed salad by searching your pantry shelf. Mix in corn or black beans, crumbled tortilla chips or croutons, dried fruits, mandarin orange segments or nuts.

Vegetable Pasta Bake

Prep time: 10 minutes   Baking time: 20 minutes

Makes 6 servings

1   jar (26 to 28 ounces) spaghetti sauce

3   cups rotini *or* penne pasta, cooked, drained

1   package (16 ounces) frozen vegetable blend, thawed

¾   cup KRAFT 100% Grated Parmesan Cheese, divided

1   package (8 ounces) KRAFT Shredded Low-Moisture Part-Skim Mozzarella Cheese

Mix spaghetti sauce, pasta, vegetables and ½ cup of the Parmesan cheese.

Spoon into 13×9-inch (3-quart) baking dish. Top with mozzarella cheese and remaining ¼ cup Parmesan cheese.

Bake at 375°F for 20 minutes.

Italian Pasta Bake

Prepare Vegetable Pasta Bake as directed, omitting vegetables. Stir in 1 pound drained cooked ground beef with spaghetti sauce.

Marshmallow Cereal Squares

Prep time: 10 minutes   Microwaving time: 2¼ minutes

Makes 2 dozen

¼ **cup (½ stick) butter *or* margarine**
1 **package (10½ ounces) miniature marshmallows (6 cups)**
8 **cups POST ALPHA-BITS Frosted Letter Shaped Oat and Corn Cereal *or* POST GOLDEN CRISP Sweetened Puffed Wheat Cereal**

Microwave butter in 4-quart microwavable bowl on HIGH 45 seconds or until melted. Add marshmallows; mix to coat. Microwave 1½ minutes or until marshmallows are melted and smooth, stirring after 45 seconds.

Add cereal; mix to coat well.

Press firmly into greased foil-lined 13×9-inch pan. Cool; cut into squares.

Peanut Butter
Chocolate
Clusters

Marshmallow
Cereal
Squares

Peanut Butter *Chocolate* Clusters

Prep time: 5 minutes plus refrigerating Microwaving time: 2 minutes

Makes about 2½ dozen

1   **package (4 ounces) BAKER'S GERMAN'S Sweet Baking Chocolate**
2   **tablespoons creamy peanut butter**
2½ **cups POST GOLDEN CRISP Sweetened Puffed Wheat Cereal**

Microwave chocolate and peanut butter in large microwavable bowl on HIGH 1½ to 2 minutes or until chocolate is almost melted, stirring halfway through heating time. Stir until chocolate is completely melted. Stir in cereal.

Drop by teaspoonfuls onto wax paper.

Refrigerate until firm. Store in tightly covered container in refrigerator.

Cream Cheese and Crackers

Think of PHILADELPHIA Cream Cheese and crackers as the mainstays in your collection of tasty snacks to take to a potluck or to serve at home. Mix and match according to your mood, starting with Apple-Cinnamon Flavor Cream Cheese on bagel chips, Strawberry Flavor on wheat crackers and Blueberry Flavor on graham crackers.

Strawberry Shortcut

Prep time: 10 minutes

Makes 7 servings

1 **package (12 ounces) pound cake, cut into 14 slices**
3 **cups strawberries, sliced, sweetened**
3½ **cups (8 ounces) thawed COOL WHIP Whipped Topping**

Place 7 of the cake slices on individual dessert plates.

Spoon about 3 tablespoons of the strawberries over each cake slice. Top each with ¼ cup whipped topping. Repeat layers. Serve immediately.

Note: Slice the pound cake and berries before you leave home, then pack separately. At the potluck, let guests make their own shortcakes.

Fruits and Vegetables

Summertime is ripe with juicy, fresh fruits and vegetables—all good for you to eat. Encourage your family to eat at least 5 servings a day for vitamins, minerals and other health benefits.

Sour Cream *Poppy Seed* Cake

Prep time: 15 minutes   Baking time: 55 minutes plus cooling

Makes 12 servings

1   **package (2-layer size) yellow cake mix, any variety**
1   **package (4-serving size) JELL-O Vanilla Flavor Instant Pudding & Pie Filling**
4   **eggs**
1   **cup BREAKSTONE'S *or* KNUDSEN Sour Cream**
½   **cup oil**
½   **cup orange juice *or* water**
¼   **cup poppy seed**

Beat cake mix, pudding mix, eggs, sour cream, oil and juice in large bowl with electric mixer on low speed just to moisten, scraping sides of bowl often. Beat on medium speed 2 minutes. Stir in poppy seed.

Spoon into greased and floured 12-cup fluted tube pan or 10-inch tube pan.

Bake at 350°F for 50 to 55 minutes or until toothpick inserted near center comes out clean. Cool 10 minutes; loosen from sides of pan with spatula or knife and gently remove cake. Cool completely on wire rack. Sprinkle with powdered sugar, if desired.

Add a Glaze

Decorate Sour Cream Poppy Seed Cake with an easy glaze. Mix 1½ cups sifted powdered sugar and 3 tablespoons milk; drizzle over the cake.

Triple Chocolate Cake

Prep time: 10 minutes   Baking time: 50 minutes plus cooling

Makes 12 servings

1 package (2-layer size) chocolate cake
    mix, any variety
1 package (4-serving size) JELL-O
    Chocolate Flavor Instant Pudding &
    Pie Filling
4 eggs
1 cup BREAKSTONE'S *or* KNUDSEN Sour
    Cream
½ cup oil
½ cup water
1½ cups miniature semi-sweet chocolate
    chips
    COOL WHIP Whipped Topping, thawed

Beat cake mix, pudding mix, eggs, sour cream, oil and water with electric mixer on low speed just to moisten, scraping sides of bowl often. Beat on medium speed 2 minutes. Stir in chips.

Spoon into greased and floured 12-cup fluted tube pan or 10-inch tube pan.

Bake at 350°F for 50 minutes or until toothpick inserted near center comes out clean. Cool 10 minutes; loosen from sides of pan with spatula or knife and gently remove cake. Cool completely on wire rack. Top each serving with whipped topping.

BAKER'S® ONE BOWL *Cream Cheese* Brownies

Prep time: 15 minutes   Baking time: 40 minutes

Makes 24 fudgy brownies

- **4** squares BAKER'S Unsweetened Baking Chocolate
- **¾** cup (1½ sticks) butter *or* margarine
- **2½** cups sugar, divided
- **5** eggs, divided
- **1¼** cups flour, divided
- **1** package (8 ounces) PHILADELPHIA Cream Cheese, softened

Heat oven to 350°F (325°F for glass baking dish). Grease foil-lined 13×9-inch baking pan.

Microwave chocolate and butter in large microwavable bowl on HIGH 2 minutes or until butter is melted. Stir until chocolate is completely melted.

Stir 2 cups of the sugar into chocolate until well blended. Mix in 4 of the eggs. Stir in 1 cup of the flour until well blended. Spread batter in pan. Beat cream cheese, remaining ½ cup sugar, 1 egg and ¼ cup flour in same bowl with wire whisk until well blended. Spoon mixture over brownie batter. Swirl batters with teaspoon to marbleize.

Bake 40 minutes or until toothpick inserted in center comes out with fudgy crumbs. DO NOT OVERBAKE. Cool in pan.

How to Melt Chocolate on Top of the Stove

Instead of microwaving the chocolate and butter as directed for BAKER'S® ONE BOWL Cream Cheese Brownies, melt chocolate and butter in heavy 3-quart saucepan on very low heat, stirring constantly until just melted. Remove from heat. Continue as directed.

BBQ Bacon Cheeseburger
(recipe, page 148) and
Great American Potato
Salad (recipe, page 199)

SUMMER CELEBRATIONS

Sometimes you don't need an occasion to have a celebration. Why not gather together with loved ones just because it is summertime? This chapter gives you some great ideas for planning that Backyard Barbecue for the neighbors or your annual Family Reunion Feast. From BLT Dip to munch on while you grill to Lemonade Stand Pie to savor after dinner, you'll find recipes and tips for creating a memorable meal.

Backyard BBQ

VELVEETA® Salsa Dip
BBQ Bacon Cheeseburgers
Easy Wrap Sandwiches
Grilled Ranch Chicken Salad
JELL-O® Strawberry Gelatin Pops
JELL-O® Creamy Chocolate Pudding Pops
JELL-O® Frozen No Bake Peanut Butter Cups
PHILADELPHIA® Cheesecake Creme Parfaits

BBQ Bacon *Cheeseburgers*

(Photo on pages 146–147.)

Prep time: 15 minutes   Grilling time: 18 minutes

Makes 4

1 **pound ground beef**
2 **tablespoons KRAFT Original Barbecue Sauce**
8 **KRAFT DELI DELUXE Process American Cheese Slices**
4 **Kaiser rolls *or* hamburger buns, split, toasted**
   Lettuce
8 **slices OSCAR MAYER Bacon, crisply cooked**

MIx meat and barbecue sauce. Shape into 4 patties.

Place patties on grill over medium coals. Grill 7 to 9 minutes on each side or until cooked through (160°F), turning and brushing occasionally with additional barbecue sauce.

Top each patty with 2 process cheese slices. Continue grilling until process cheese begins to melt. Fill rolls with lettuce, cheeseburgers and bacon.

VELVEETA® Salsa *Dip*

Prep time: 5 minutes   Microwaving time: 5 minutes

Makes 3 cups

**1   pound (16 ounces) VELVEETA Pasteurized
      Prepared Cheese Product, cut up**
**1   cup TACO BELL HOME ORIGINALS Thick 'N
      Chunky Salsa**

Microwave prepared cheese product and salsa in 1½-quart microwavable bowl on HIGH 5 minutes or until prepared cheese product is melted, stirring after 3 minutes. Garnish with pepper knots. Serve hot with assorted tortilla chips or cut-up vegetables.

TACO BELL and HOME ORIGINALS are registered trademarks owned and licensed by Taco Bell Corp.

Easy Wrap Sandwiches

(Photo on page 158.)

KRAFT Mayo Real Mayonnaise *or*
 MIRACLE WHIP Salad Dressing
Flour tortilla
Lettuce
OSCAR MAYER Smoked Cooked Ham
KRAFT Singles
CLAUSSEN Kosher Dill Sandwich Slices

Spread mayo on tortilla.

Top with lettuce, ham, Singles and pickles. Fold up sides of tortilla to center, slightly overlapping. Secure with garnished toothpick, if desired.

Easy Wrap Sandwiches with Turkey

Prepare Easy Wrap Sandwiches as directed, except substitute LOUIS RICH Oven Roasted Turkey Breast for ham and TACO BELL HOME ORIGINALS Thick 'N Chunky Salsa for pickles.

TACO BELL and HOME ORIGINALS are registered trademarks owned and licensed by Taco Bell Corp.

Grilled Ranch *Chicken* Salad

Prep time: 15 minutes   Grilling time: 15 minutes

Makes 6 servings

1   **pound boneless skinless chicken breast
      halves**
½   **cup KRAFT Original Barbecue Sauce**
1   **package (10 ounces) salad greens**
1   **large tomato, cut into wedges**
½   **cup sliced red onion**
½   **cup KRAFT Ranch Dressing**
¼   **cup crumbled blue cheese**

Place chicken on greased grill over medium coals. Grill 12 to 15 minutes or until cooked through (160°F), turning and brushing occasionally with barbecue sauce. Cool slightly; slice chicken.

Toss greens, tomato and onion in large bowl. Pour dressing over greens mixture. Serve chicken over greens mixture. Sprinkle with cheese.

JELL-O® *Strawberry* Gelatin Pops

(Photo on page 155.)

Prep time: 10 minutes   Freezing time: 5 hours

Makes 6

1   **cup boiling water**
1   **package (4-serving size) JELL-O Brand**
    Strawberry Flavor Gelatin
⅓   **cup sugar**
1⅓ **cups cold water**

Stir boiling water into gelatin and sugar in medium bowl at least 2 minutes until completely dissolved. Stir in cold water.

Pour into 5-ounce paper cups. Insert pop stick into each cup for handle.

Freeze 5 hours or overnight until firm. To remove pops from cups, place bottoms of cups under warm running water for 15 seconds. Press firmly on bottoms of cups to release pops. (Do not twist or pull pop sticks.) Store leftover pops in freezer.

Chilling Made Easy

Having a big backyard party? Use a kiddie swimming pool filled with ice as a large cooler. Set it alongside the buffet table to keep pitchers and cans of beverages well chilled. Or, if you have a large buffet table, put the ice-filled pool on your table and nestle bowls of salads in the ice.

JELL-O® Creamy *Chocolate* Pudding Pops

Prep time: 10 minutes   Freezing time: 5 hours

Makes 6

2   **cups cold milk**
1   **package (4-serving size) JELL-O Chocolate Flavor Instant Pudding & Pie Filling**
1   **cup thawed COOL WHIP Whipped Topping**

Pour cold milk into medium bowl. Add pudding mix. Beat with wire whisk 1 minute. Stir in whipped topping.

Spoon into 5-ounce paper cups. Insert pop stick into each cup for handle.

Freeze 5 hours or overnight until firm. To remove pops from cups, place bottoms of cups under warm running water for 15 seconds. Press firmly on bottoms of cups to release pops. (Do not twist or pull pop sticks.) Store leftover pops in freezer.

JELL-O® Strawberry
Gelatin Pops (recipe,
page 153) and JELL-O®
Creamy Chocolate
Pudding Pops (recipe,
opposite)

JELL-O® *Frozen* No Bake Peanut Butter Cups

Prep time: 15 minutes   Freezing time: 2 hours

Makes 12 to 15 cups

1 **package (16.1 ounces) JELL-O No Bake Peanut Butter Cup Dessert**
⅓ **cup melted margarine**
1⅓ **cups cold milk**

Mix Crust Mix as directed on package in medium bowl. Press onto bottoms of 12 to 15 foil-cup-lined muffin cups (about 1 heaping tablespoon per muffin cup).

Prepare Filling Mix as directed on package in deep, medium bowl. Divide filling among muffin cups. Place Topping Pouch in hot water 30 seconds. Knead pouch 30 seconds. Squeeze topping equally over cups. Freeze 2 hours or until firm. Store, covered, in freezer up to 2 weeks.

JELL-O® Frozen No Bake Cookies & Creme Cups: Prepare JELL-O No Bake Double Layer Cookies & Creme Dessert as directed on package, pressing prepared crust mixture onto bottoms of 12 foil-cup-lined muffin cups. Divide prepared filling mixture among cups. Top with reserved cookies. Freeze and store as directed above. Makes 12.

JELL-O® Frozen
No Bake Cookies
& Creme Cups and
JELL-O® Frozen
No Bake Peanut
Butter Cups

PHILADELPHIA® Cheesecake Creme *Parfaits*

Prep time: 5 minutes plus refrigerating

Makes 4 servings

1 **package (8 ounces) PHILADELPHIA Cream Cheese, softened**
1 **jar (7 ounces) marshmallow creme**
1 **cup *each* sliced strawberries and blueberries**

Mix cream cheese and marshmallow creme until well blended. Refrigerate.

Layer fruit with cream cheese mixture in dessert dishes or wine glasses. Garnish with fresh mint leaves and orange slice.

Easy Wrap Sandwich
(recipe, page 150) and
Crunchy Bacon Coleslaw
(recipe, page 161)

Potluck Picnic

Caesar Dip
Easy Taco Salad
Simple Summer Marinade
Easy Wrap Sandwiches (recipe, page 150)
Crunchy Bacon Coleslaw
Quick Vanilla Rice Pudding
JELL-O® Frozen Pudding and Gelatin Snacks
PHILADELPHIA® No-Bake Cheesecake

Caesar Dip

Prep time: 10 minutes

Makes 2 cups

1 **package (8 ounces) PHILADELPHIA Cream Cheese, softened**
1 **cup KRAFT 100% Grated Parmesan Cheese**
½ **cup KRAFT Classic Caesar Dressing**
1 **cup chopped romaine lettuce**
½ **cup croutons**

Beat cream cheese, Parmesan cheese and dressing with electric mixer on medium speed until well blended.

Spread on bottom of 9-inch pie plate. Top with lettuce and croutons. Sprinkle with additional Parmesan cheese, if desired. Garnish with lemon wedges. Serve with assorted crackers.

Easy Taco Salad

Prep time: 10 minutes   Cooking time: 10 minutes

Makes 4 servings

1	**pound ground beef**
½	**cup TACO BELL HOME ORIGINALS Thick 'N Chunky Salsa**
4	**cups shredded lettuce**
	Tortilla chips
1	**cup KRAFT Four Cheese Mexican Style Shredded Cheese**

Brown meat; drain. Stir in salsa.

Layer lettuce, chips, meat mixture and cheese on large platter or individual serving plates. Top with chopped tomato and sour cream, if desired. Garnish with green onion curls.

TACO BELL and HOME ORIGINALS are registered trademarks owned and licensed by Taco Bell Corp.

Crunchy Bacon *Coleslaw*

(Photo on pages 158 and 195.)

Prep time: 15 minutes plus refrigerating

Makes 10 servings or about 4 cups

¾ **cup MIRACLE WHIP *or* MIRACLE WHIP LIGHT Dressing**
1 **tablespoon sugar**
1½ **teaspoons cider vinegar**
4 **cups shredded green cabbage**
1 **cup shredded red cabbage**
½ **cup chopped peanuts**
4 **slices OSCAR MAYER Bacon, crisply cooked, crumbled**

Mix dressing, sugar and vinegar in large bowl.

Add remaining ingredients; mix lightly. Refrigerate. Serve in lettuce-lined bowl.

Quick Crunchy Bacon Coleslaw

Prepare Crunchy Bacon Coleslaw as directed, except substitute 1 package (8 ounces) coleslaw blend for shredded green and red cabbage. Substitute 1 can (3 ounces) OSCAR MAYER Real Bacon Bits for bacon slices.

Simple Summer Marinade

Prep time: 10 minutes plus marinating   Grilling time: 40 minutes

Makes 4 servings

1   envelope **GOOD SEASONS Salad Dressing Mix, any variety**
1   **broiler-fryer chicken, cut up (3 to 3½ pounds)**

Prepare salad dressing mix as directed on envelope.

Pour over chicken; cover. Refrigerate several hours to overnight to marinate. Drain, discarding dressing.

Place chicken on greased grill over medium coals. Grill, covered, 35 to 40 minutes or until chicken is cooked through (160°F), turning occasionally.

Marinate Before Work, Cook Out Tonight

When you have a potluck or picnic to attend after work, refrigerate the poultry or meat in a marinade, such as Simple Summer Marinade, in the morning. Before you eat, all you'll need to do is light the coals and grill. This works great for everyday family meals, too.

Quick Vanilla Rice Pudding

Prep time: 5 minutes   Cooking time: 10 minutes plus standing

Makes 6 servings

3 cups milk, divided
1 cup MINUTE White Rice, uncooked
⅓ cup raisins
**1 package (4-serving size) JELL-O Vanilla
    Flavor Instant Pudding & Pie Filling**

Boil 1 cup of the milk. Stir in rice and raisins; cover. Let stand 5 minutes.

Meanwhile, prepare pudding as directed on package with remaining 2 cups milk.

Add rice mixture to prepared pudding; stir. Cover surface of pudding with plastic wrap; cool 5 minutes. Stir. Serve warm or chilled. Sprinkle with cinnamon and garnish with cookies, if desired. Store leftover rice pudding in refrigerator.

JELL-O® Frozen Pudding and Gelatin *Snacks*

Freezing time: 5 hours

Remove foil lid from JELL-O Pudding *or* Gelatin Snack. Insert pop stick into pudding or gelatin cup for handle. Freeze 5 hours or overnight until firm. To remove pop from cup, place bottom of cup under warm running water for 15 seconds. Press firmly on bottom of cup to release pop. (Do not twist or pull pop stick.) Once thawed, pops do not refreeze or refrigerate well.

PHILADELPHIA® *No-Bake* Cheesecake

Prep time: 10 minutes plus refrigerating

Makes 8 servings

1 **package (8 ounces) PHILADELPHIA Cream Cheese, softened**

⅓ **cup sugar**

1 **tub (8 ounces) COOL WHIP Whipped Topping, thawed**

1 **prepared graham cracker crumb crust (6 ounce *or* 9 inch)**

Mix cream cheese and sugar with electric mixer on medium speed until well blended. Gently stir in whipped topping.

Spoon into crust. Refrigerate 3 hours or overnight. Top with fresh fruit or cherry pie filling, if desired. Store leftover cheesecake in refrigerator.

Removing from Foil Pan

If you prefer to serve PHILADELPHIA® No-Bake Cheesecake in your own pie plate rather than in the foil pan, use kitchen shears to carefully cut foil pan. Then, peel pan from crust and place cheesecake in pie plate.

Chicken Sour Cream
Enchiladas (recipe, page
170)

Southwestern Fiesta

VELVEETA® Ranch Dip
Mexi-Style Roll-Ups
Chicken Sour Cream Enchiladas
Salsa Macaroni 'n Cheese
Southwestern Grilled Chicken Salad
COOL 'N EASY® Pie
Easy Lemon Berry Dessert

VELVEETA® Ranch *Dip*

Prep time: 5 minutes Microwaving time: 5 minutes

Makes 3 cups

1   pound (16 ounces) VELVEETA Pasteurized
    Prepared Cheese Product, cut up
1   container (8 ounces) BREAKSTONE'S *or*
    KNUDSEN Sour Cream
1   cup KRAFT Ranch Dressing

Microwave prepared cheese product in 1½-quart microwavable bowl on HIGH 4 minutes or until melted, stirring after 2 minutes.

Stir in sour cream and dressing. Microwave 1 minute. Serve hot with tortilla chips and/or cut-up vegetables.

Chicken Sour Cream *Enchiladas*

(Photo on page 168.)

Prep time: 20 minutes Baking time: 35 minutes

Makes 5 servings

1 **container (16 ounces) BREAKSTONE'S *or* KNUDSEN Sour Cream, divided**
2 **cups chopped cooked chicken**
1 **package (8 ounces) KRAFT Natural *or* ⅓ Less Fat Shredded Reduced Fat Colby and Monterey Jack Cheese, divided**
1 **cup salsa, divided**
2 **tablespoons chopped fresh cilantro**
1 **teaspoon ground cumin**
10 **flour tortillas (6 inch)**
1 **cup shredded lettuce**
½ **cup chopped tomato**

Mix 1 cup of the sour cream, chicken, 1 cup of the cheese, ¼ cup of the salsa, cilantro and cumin.

Spoon about ¼ cup of the chicken mixture down center of each tortilla; roll up. Place, seam side down, in 13×9-inch (3-quart) baking dish. Top with remaining ¾ cup salsa; cover.

Bake at 350°F for 30 minutes. Sprinkle with remaining 1 cup cheese. Bake an additional 5 minutes or until cheese is melted. Top with lettuce and tomato. Serve with remaining 1 cup sour cream.

Mexi-Style Roll-Ups

Serve these easy tortilla roll-ups as an appetizer. For a special touch, garnish with red grapes.

- Spread flour tortillas with KRAFT, BREAKSTONE'S *or* KNUDSEN FREE Fat Free Creamy Salsa Dip.

- Top with slices of LOUIS RICH Oven Roasted Turkey Breast or LOUIS RICH CARVING BOARD Thin Carved Honey Glazed Ham and shredded lettuce.

- Roll up tortillas. Secure with toothpicks. Slice into 1-inch pieces.

Salsa Macaroni 'n Cheese

Prep time: 10 minutes   Cooking time: 15 minutes

Makes 6 servings

1   **pound ground beef**
1   **jar (16 ounces) chunky salsa**
1½ **cups water**
1   **package (7 ounces) elbow macaroni, uncooked**
¾   **pound (12 ounces) VELVEETA Pasteurized Prepared Cheese Product, cut up**

Brown meat in large skillet; drain.

Stir in salsa and water. Bring to boil.

Stir in macaroni. Reduce heat to medium-low; cover. Simmer 8 to 10 minutes or until macaroni is tender.

Add prepared cheese product; stir until melted. Garnish with red pepper rings and fresh oregano.

Southwestern *Grilled* Chicken Salad

Prep time: 20 minutes   Grilling time: 15 minutes

Makes 4 servings

1   **pound boneless skinless chicken breast halves**
8   **cups shredded lettuce**
1   **cup KRAFT Four Cheese Mexican Style Shredded Cheese**
1   **large tomato, cut into wedges**
½   **cup canned black beans, drained, rinsed**
¼   **cup sliced green onions**

Place chicken on greased grill over medium coals. Grill 12 to 15 minutes or until cooked through (160°F), turning once. Cool chicken slightly; cut into ¼-inch slices.

Arrange all ingredients on large serving platter.

Serve with KRAFT Ranch Dressing or salsa.

Tomato Tips

- If you're shopping for tomatoes, roll them between the palms of your hands—they should give a little when perfectly ripe. Ripe tomatoes should not feel soggy or have broken skins.

- Store ripe tomatoes in a cool place or in your refrigerator vegetable crisper for up to 5 days. Try to use them as soon as possible, while their flavor and texture are at their peak. Do not refrigerate unripe tomatoes because that will halt the ripening process. Ripen unripe tomatoes in a brown paper bag or fruit-ripening bowl for a few days.

COOL 'N EASY® *Pie*

Prep time: 10 minutes   Refrigerating time: 4 hours and 20 minutes

Makes 8 servings

⅔ **cup boiling water**

1 **package (4-serving size) JELL-O Brand Gelatin, any flavor**

½ **cup cold water**
  Ice cubes

1 **tub (8 ounces) COOL WHIP Whipped Topping, thawed**

1 **prepared graham cracker crumb crust (6 ounce *or* 9 inch)**
  Fruit (optional)

Stir boiling water into gelatin in large bowl at least 2 minutes until completely dissolved. Mix cold water and ice to make ¾ cup. Add to gelatin, stirring until slightly thickened. Remove any remaining ice.

Stir in whipped topping with wire whisk until smooth. Refrigerate 15 to 20 minutes or until mixture is very thick and will mound. Spoon into crust.

Refrigerate 4 hours or overnight. Just before serving, top with fruit. Store leftover pie in refrigerator.

Easy Lemon Berry Dessert

Prep time: 5 minutes plus refrigerating

Makes 6 servings

1   **tub (8 ounces) COOL WHIP Whipped Topping, thawed**
1   **tablespoon grated lemon peel**
1   **package (5 ounces) sponge cake *or* dessert shells**
2   **cups sliced strawberries**

Mix whipped topping and lemon peel in large bowl until well blended. Refrigerate until ready to serve.

Spoon whipped topping mixture over sponge cake. Top with strawberries.

BLT Dip (recipe, opposite)

Fabulous 4th Cookout

BLT *Dip*

Prep time: 20 minutes plus refrigerating

Makes 12 servings

1   container (16 ounces) BREAKSTONE'S *or*
    KNUDSEN Sour Cream
1   package (16 ounces) OSCAR MAYER
    Bacon, cooked, crumbled
1½ teaspoons onion salt
½   cup KRAFT Shredded Cheddar Cheese
1   tomato, chopped, divided
1   cup shredded lettuce

Mix sour cream, bacon and onion salt.

Spoon into bottom of 1-quart star-shaped dish or 9-inch pie plate.

Top with cheese, 3/4 cup of the chopped tomato, lettuce and remaining chopped tomato. Refrigerate. Serve with crackers.

Summer Coolers

Here are a few thirst-quenching drinks that are great for the 4th of July or anytime.

- Mix prepared TANG with softened vanilla ice cream for a dreamy orange drink.
- Stir 2 tablespoons KOOL-AID mix into 8 ounces seltzer water for a fun soda.
- Pour prepared TANG or KOOL-AID over scoops of fruit sherbet or sorbet.

Asian Honey BBQ Chicken *Drummettes*

Prep time: 10 minutes   Grilling time: 15 minutes

Makes 15 appetizers

1   cup **KRAFT Honey Barbecue Sauce**
1½ tablespoons **soy sauce**
½   teaspoon **ground ginger**
¼   teaspoon **garlic powder**
15 **chicken drummettes (about 1½ pounds)**

Mix barbecue sauce, soy sauce, ginger and garlic powder.

Place chicken on greased grill over medium coals.

Grill 15 minutes or until chicken is cooked through (160°F), turning and brushing occasionally with barbecue sauce mixture. Serve with additional barbecue sauce, if desired.

Cajun BBQ Franks

Prep time: 5 minutes   Grilling time: 10 minutes

Makes 8

2 **CLAUSSEN Whole Kosher Dill Pickles, chopped (about ½ cup)**
½ **cup KRAFT THICK 'N SPICY Spicy Cajun Barbecue Sauce**
¼ **red pepper, chopped (about ¼ cup)**
2 **tablespoons chopped onion**
8 **OSCAR MAYER Beef Franks *or* Wieners**
8 **hot dog buns**

Mix pickles, barbecue sauce, red pepper and onion.

Grill franks until thoroughly heated (160°F), turning occasionally.

Place franks in buns; top with pickle mixture.

Note: You can make the pickle mixture a day ahead, then refrigerate until ready to serve.

Spicy Cajun BBQ Franks

Prepare Cajun BBQ Franks as directed, adding ¼ teaspoon crushed red pepper to pickle mixture.

Turkey-in-the-Round *Sandwich*

Prep time: 10 minutes

Makes 8 servings

1   **loaf (about 24 ounces) round Italian bread**
    MIRACLE WHIP Salad Dressing *or* KRAFT Mayo Real Mayonnaise
    Lettuce leaves
    Tomato slices
1   **package (5.5 ounces) LOUIS RICH CARVING BOARD Oven Roasted Turkey Breast**
4   **KRAFT Singles, cut in half**

Cut bread in half horizontally.

Spread cut surfaces of bread with salad dressing.

Layer bottom half of bread with lettuce, tomato, turkey and Singles. Cover with top half of bread. Cut into wedges.

Tangy *Broccoli* Salad

(Photo on page 183.)

Prep time: 20 minutes plus refrigerating

Makes 8 servings

1   cup MIRACLE WHIP *or* MIRACLE WHIP LIGHT Dressing
2   tablespoons *each* sugar and vinegar
1   medium bunch broccoli, cut into flowerets (about 6 cups)
12 slices OSCAR MAYER Bacon, crisply cooked, crumbled
½   cup chopped red onion

Mix dressing, sugar and vinegar in large bowl.

Add remaining ingredients; mix lightly. Refrigerate.

Leafy Broccoli Salad

Prepare Tangy Broccoli Salad as directed, adding 4 cups loosely packed torn lettuce or spinach leaves.

Mediterranean Pasta Salad

Prep time: 25 minutes

Makes 6 to 8 servings

1 package (9.15 ounces) KRAFT 97% Fat Free Italian Pasta Salad
1 cup chopped seeded cucumber
½ cup chopped tomato
¼ cup thinly sliced red onion
¼ cup crumbled ATHENOS Feta Cheese (optional)

Prepare Pasta Salad as directed on package.

Stir in remaining ingredients. Serve immediately or refrigerate.

Caribbean Jerk Chicken (recipe, page 44) Mediterranean Pasta Salad (recipe, opposite) and Tangy Broccoli Salad (recipe, page 181)

Lemonade Stand Pie

Prep time: 15 minutes Freezing time: 4 hours

Makes 8 servings

⅓ cup COUNTRY TIME Lemonade Flavor
    Drink Mix *or* COUNTRY TIME LEM'N
    BERRY SIPPERS Drink Mix, any flavor

½ cup water

1 pint vanilla ice cream (2 cups),
   softened

1 tub (8 ounces) COOL WHIP Whipped
   Topping, thawed

1 prepared graham cracker crumb crust
   (6 ounce *or* 9 inch)

Stir drink mix and water until dissolved.

Beat lemonade mixture and ice cream in large bowl with electric mixer on low speed until well blended. Gently stir in whipped topping until smooth. Freeze until mixture will mound, if necessary. Spoon into crust.

Freeze 4 hours or overnight until firm. Let stand at room temperature 15 minutes or until pie can be cut easily. Garnish with lemon slices, if desired. Store leftover pie in freezer.

Easy American Dessert

Prep time: 20 minutes   Refrigerating time: 4 hours

Makes 12 to 15 servings

4   cups boiling water
**1   package (8-serving size) *or* 2 packages
      (4-serving size *each*) JELL-O Brand
      Gelatin, any red flavor**
**1   package (8-serving size) *or* 2 packages
      (4-serving size *each*) JELL-O Brand
      Berry Blue Flavor Gelatin**
2   cups cold water
4   cups cubed pound cake
**1   tub (8 ounces) COOL WHIP Whipped
      Topping, thawed**
**2   cups sliced strawberries *or* 3 medium
      bananas, sliced**

Stir 2 cups of the boiling water into each flavor of gelatin in separate bowls at least 2 minutes until completely dissolved. Stir 1 cup of the cold water into each bowl. Pour into separate 13×9-inch pans. Refrigerate 3 hours or until firm. Cut gelatin into 1/2-inch cubes.

Place red gelatin cubes in 31/2-quart bowl or trifle bowl. Layer with cake cubes, 1/2 of the whipped topping and strawberries. Cover with blue gelatin cubes. Top with remaining whipped topping.

Refrigerate at least 1 hour or until ready to serve. Store leftover dessert in refrigerator.

4th-of-July *Cheesecake*

Prep time: 20 minutes plus refrigerating

Makes 12 servings

1½ **cups graham cracker crumbs**
½   **cup (1 stick) butter *or* margarine, melted**
¼   **cup granulated sugar**
2   **packages (8 ounces *each*) PHILADELPHIA Cream Cheese, softened**
2   **cups powdered sugar**
1   **tub (8 ounces) COOL WHIP Whipped Topping, thawed**
    Strawberry jam, heated
    Blueberries

Mix crumbs, butter and granulated sugar. Press onto bottom of 13×9-inch dish.

Beat cream cheese and powdered sugar with electric mixer on medium speed until well blended. Gently stir in whipped topping. Spoon cream cheese mixture over crust. Refrigerate 1 hour or overnight.

Press star cookie cutters lightly into top of cheesecake. Drizzle warm jam to cover remaining surface of cheesecake. Carefully remove cookie cutters. Arrange blueberries around edge of cheesecake. Store leftover cheesecake in refrigerator.

Mock Sangria

Prep time: 10 minutes plus refrigerating

Makes 1 gallon or 16 servings

1 envelope (2-quart size) KOOL-AID ISLAND TWISTS Orange-Pineapple Flavor Sugar-Sweetened Soft Drink Mix *or* KOOL-AID Strawberry Kiwi Flavor Sugar-Sweetened Soft Drink Mix *or* KOOL-AID Orange Flavor Sugar-Sweetened Soft Drink Mix

4 cups cold water

4 cups ice cubes

5 cups assorted fruit (sliced carambola, lemons, oranges and strawberries, raspberries *or* canned pineapple tidbits, drained)

1 bottle (25.4 ounces) chilled non-alcoholic sparkling red grape juice

2 cups chilled ginger ale

Pour soft drink mix into large bowl or punch bowl. Add water and ice cubes; stir to dissolve.

Stir in fruit. Refrigerate. Just before serving, stir in non-alcoholic sparkling red grape juice and ginger ale.

Note: Do not prepare or store this beverage in a metal container.

Strawberry Hints

When you're selecting strawberries, make sure to choose the plumpest, reddest, most fully ripened strawberries you can find, because they don't ripen after they are picked. And remember, the biggest berries are not necessarily the sweetest and juiciest. The smaller ones—as long as they're not bruised, wet or mushy—can be just as sweet as the bigger ones.

Once you have them home from the supermarket, store strawberries in a single layer, loosely covered, in the refrigerator. Because strawberries are highly perishable, they should be used within 1 to 2 days. Just before you're ready to use them, wash and hull the berries.

Hot Artichoke Dip
(recipe, opposite)

Family Reunion Feast

Hot Artichoke Dip
Easy Italian Dip
Super Crunch Burgers
Grilled Salsa Chicken
Crunchy Bacon Coleslaw (recipe, page 161)
Three Bean Salad
Great American Potato Salad
Toffee Bar Dessert
BAKER'S® ONE BOWL Chocolate Chocolate Chunk Cookies
Hot Coffee Float
Iced Chocolaccino

Hot *Artichoke* Dip

Prep time: 10 minutes   Baking time: 25 minutes

Makes 2 cups

1   **can (14 ounces) artichoke hearts, drained, chopped**
1   **cup KRAFT 100% Grated Parmesan Cheese**
1   **cup KRAFT Mayo Real Mayonnaise *or* MIRACLE WHIP Salad Dressing**
1   **clove garlic, minced**
    Chopped tomato
    Sliced fresh chives

Mix all ingredients except tomato and chives.

Spoon into 9-inch pie plate or quiche dish.

Bake at 350°F for 20 to 25 minutes or until lightly browned. Sprinkle with tomato and chives. Serve with crackers.

Note: To make Hot Artichoke Dip ahead, prepare as directed except do not bake; cover. Refrigerate overnight. Before serving, bake, uncovered, at 350°F for 20 to 25 minutes or until lightly browned.

Variations

Spicy Artichoke Dip: Prepare Hot Artichoke Dip as directed, adding 1 can (4 ounces) chopped green chilies, drained.

Spinach Artichoke Dip: Prepare Hot Artichoke Dip as directed, adding 1 package (10 ounces) frozen chopped spinach, thawed, well drained.

Easy Italian *Dip*

Prep time: 5 minutes plus refrigerating

Makes 2 cups

1 **container (16 ounces) BREAKSTONE'S or KNUDSEN Sour Cream**

1 **envelope GOOD SEASONS Basil Vinaigrette or Italian Salad Dressing Mix**

Mix sour cream and salad dressing mix.

Stir in 1 other suggested ingredient (see tip below), if desired. Refrigerate. Serve with breadsticks and assorted cut-up vegetables.

Add an Extra

To add your personal touch to Easy Italian Dip, stir in any one of the following ingredients:

- ¼ cup sun-dried tomatoes in olive oil, drained, chopped
- ½ cup chopped roasted red pepper
- 1 teaspoon jarred roasted garlic
- 1 can (8½ ounces) artichoke hearts, drained, finely chopped

Super Crunch Burgers

Prep time: 15 minutes   Grilling time: 18 minutes

Makes 4

1½ **pounds ground beef**
¼ **cup KRAFT Mayo Real Mayonnaise**
1 **tablespoon Dijon mustard**
4 **Kaiser rolls *or* hamburger buns, split, toasted**
4 **to 8 CLAUSSEN Super Slices For Burgers**

Shape meat into 4 patties.

Place patties on grill over medium coals. Grill 7 to 9 minutes on each side or until cooked through (160°F).

Mix mayo and mustard; spread on cut surfaces of rolls. Place patties on rolls; top with pickle slices.

Super Stuffed Burgers

Shape meat for Super Crunch Burgers into 8 thin patties. Top 4 patties each with 1 tablespoon ATHENOS Crumbled Basil & Tomato Feta Cheese and a second patty. Pinch edges of patties together to seal. Continue as directed for Super Crunch Burgers.

Super Crunch Burger
(recipe, opposite) and
Crunchy Bacon Coleslaw
(recipe, page 161)

Grilled Salsa Chicken
(recipe, opposite) and
Three Bean Salad (recipe,
page 198)

Grilled Salsa Chicken

Prep time: 15 minutes   Grilling time: 15 minutes

Makes 4 servings

**4   boneless skinless chicken breast halves
       (about 1¼ pounds)**
**1   cup TACO BELL HOME ORIGINALS Thick 'N
       Chunky Salsa, divided**
4   KRAFT Singles

Marinate chicken in ½ cup of the salsa for 15 minutes.

Place chicken on greased grill over medium coals. Grill 12 to 15 minutes or until cooked through (160°F), turning once.

Top each chicken breast half with 1 Singles and 2 tablespoons of the salsa. Continue grilling 2 to 3 minutes or until Singles begins to melt.

TACO BELL and HOME ORIGINALS are registered trademarks owned and licensed by Taco Bell Corp.

Plan a Reunion

Who, what, where and when? The further ahead you plan, the more likely that out-of-towners can attend your reunion. First reserve a location—outdoors works best, with shelter backup in case of rain. Then, draft committees to plan food, entertainment, family history and housing, if needed.

Three Bean *Salad*

(Photo on page 196.)

Prep time: 10 minutes plus refrigerating

Makes 8 servings

1   **can (16 ounces) kidney beans, rinsed, drained**

1   **can (16 ounces) great Northern beans, rinsed, drained**

½   **pound fresh green beans, cooked**

½   **cup *each* diced red pepper and red onion**

¾   **cup SEVEN SEAS VIVA Italian Dressing**

Toss all ingredients in large bowl. Refrigerate.

Green Bean Hints

To quickly cook the green beans for Three Bean Salad, place beans in a 2-quart microwavable bowl with 2 tablespoons water. Cover. Microwave on HIGH 5 to 7 minutes or until crisp-tender.

If fresh green beans aren't available, substitute 1 package (10 ounces) frozen green beans, thawed, for fresh green beans. To quickly thaw green beans, place in a colander under running water for 2 to 3 minutes or until thawed.

Great American *Potato* Salad

(Photo on pages 146–147.)

Prep time: 20 minutes plus refrigerating

Makes 6 servings

¾ **cup MIRACLE WHIP Salad Dressing *or* KRAFT Mayo Real Mayonnaise**
1 **teaspoon mustard**
¼ **teaspoon celery seed**
4 **cups cubed cooked potatoes (about 1½ pounds)**
½ **cup *each* sweet pickle relish and sliced celery**
Salt and pepper

Mix salad dressing, mustard and celery seed in large bowl.

Add remaining ingredients; mix lightly. Season to taste with salt and pepper. Refrigerate. Garnish with lettuce leaves.

Toffee Bar Dessert

Prep time: 20 minutes plus refrigerating   Baking time: 10 minutes

Makes 15 servings

1   **cup flour**
½   **cup pecans, toasted, finely chopped**
¼   **cup sugar**
½   **cup (1 stick) butter *or* margarine, melted**
1   **cup toffee bits, divided**
2   **cups cold milk**
2   **packages (4-serving size *each*) JELL-O Butterscotch Flavor Instant Pudding & Pie Filling**
1   **tub (8 ounces) COOL WHIP Whipped Topping, thawed**

Mix flour, pecans, sugar, butter and ½ cup of the toffee bits in large bowl until well mixed. Press firmly onto bottom of 13×9-inch pan. Bake at 400°F for 10 minutes or until lightly browned. Cool.

Pour milk into large bowl. Add pudding mixes. Beat with wire whisk 1 to 2 minutes or until well blended. Spread 1½ cups pudding on bottom of crust.

Gently stir ½ of the whipped topping into remaining pudding. Spread over pudding in pan. Top with remaining whipped topping. Sprinkle with remaining ½ cup toffee bits. Refrigerate 3 hours or overnight. Store leftover dessert in refrigerator.

Toffee Bar Dessert (recipe, opposite) and Hot Coffee Float (recipe, page 203)

BAKER'S® ONE BOWL
Chocolate Chocolate Chunk Cookies

Prep time: 15 minutes   Baking time: 13 minutes per batch

Makes about 1½ dozen large cookies

- **2** packages (8 squares *each*) **BAKER'S** Semi-Sweet Baking Chocolate, **divided**
- **¾** cup firmly packed brown sugar
- **¼** cup (½ stick) butter *or* margarine, softened
- **2** eggs
- **1** teaspoon vanilla
- **½** cup flour
- **¼** teaspoon CALUMET Baking Powder
- **2** cups chopped nuts (optional)

Chop coarsely 8 squares (1 package) of the chocolate; set aside.

Microwave remaining 8 squares (1 package) chocolate in large microwavable bowl on HIGH 1 to 2 minutes. Stir until chocolate is melted and smooth. Stir in sugar, butter, eggs and vanilla with wooden spoon until well blended. Stir in flour and baking powder. Stir in reserved chopped chocolate and nuts. Drop by scant ¼ cupfuls onto ungreased cookie sheets.

Bake at 350°F for 12 to 13 minutes or until cookies are puffed and feel set to the touch. Cool on cookie sheets 1 minute. Cool completely on wire racks.

Hot Coffee Float

(Photo on page 201.)

Prep time: 5 minutes

Makes 1 serving

¾ **cup (6 ounces) hot freshly brewed MAXWELL HOUSE *or* YUBAN Coffee, any variety**

1 **scoop coffee, chocolate *or* vanilla ice cream**

Pour coffee over ice cream in large cup or mug. Serve immediately.

Iced Chocolaccino

Prep time: 5 minutes plus refrigerating

Makes 6 servings

3 **envelopes (1 ounce *each*) instant hot cocoa mix**

6 **cups freshly brewed MAXWELL HOUSE *or* YUBAN Coffee, any variety Ice cubes**

Empty cocoa mix into large heatproof pitcher. Add coffee; stir until dissolved. Refrigerate until ready to serve. Serve over ice cubes in tall glasses.

Luscious Berries and
Pudding Pound Cake
(recipe, page 206)

SUMMERTIME SWEETS

C ap off summertime cookouts with these tantalizing treats. Whether your taste runs toward Luscious Berries and Pudding Pound Cake or Chocolate Cherry Cheesecake, you'll find many recipes to please in this chapter. Plus, they are simple and quick to prepare so you can treat your family and friends to great-tasting desserts often and still have time to enjoy warm-weather activities.

Luscious Berries and Pudding Pound Cake

(Photo on pages 204–205.)

Prep time: 10 minutes plus refrigerating

Makes 6 servings

1	**cup BREAKSTONE'S *or* KNUDSEN Sour Cream**
¼	**cup firmly packed brown sugar**
2	**cups strawberries, sliced**
¼	**cup strawberry preserves**
6	**slices (1 inch thick) pound cake**
1	**cup blueberries**

Mix sour cream and sugar. Refrigerate.

Toss strawberries and preserves. Let stand at room temperature 30 minutes. Spoon sour cream mixture over each pound cake slice. Top with strawberry mixture and blueberries. Serve immediately.

Make It Special

For an extra-special presentation of Luscious Berries and Pudding Pound Cake, cut pound cake into shapes with cookie cutters. Place fruit on individual plates; top with pound cake shapes and sour cream mixture. Garnish with additional fruit.

Peachy Berry Dessert

Prep time: 25 minutes

Makes 12 servings

1   **tablespoon sugar**
½   **teaspoon ground cinnamon**
½   **package (15 ounces) refrigerated pie crust (1 crust)**
1   **tablespoon butter *or* margarine, melted**
2   **cans (16 ounces *each*) peach slices in juice, undrained**
2   **packages (8 ounces *each*) PHILADELPHIA Cream Cheese, softened**
½   **cup sugar**
1   **tub (12 ounces) COOL WHIP Whipped Topping, thawed**
½   **cup sliced strawberries *or* blueberries**

Mix 1 tablespoon sugar and cinnamon. Unfold crust; cut into 12 wedges. Place pastry wedges on cookie sheet, ½ inch apart. Brush with melted butter; sprinkle with cinnamon-sugar mixture. Bake at 400°F for 8 to 10 minutes or until lightly browned.

Drain peaches, reserving ½ cup juice. Beat cream cheese and ½ cup sugar in large bowl with wire whisk until smooth. Gradually beat in reserved ½ cup juice. Gently stir in whipped topping.

Spoon into 12 individual dessert dishes. Top with peaches, strawberries and pastry wedges.

Juicy Fruited *Summer* Pie

Prep time: 10 minutes   Refrigerating time: 4 hours and 25 minutes

Makes 8 servings

⅔ **cup boiling orange-pineapple-banana juice**

1 **package (4-serving size) JELL-O Brand Pineapple *or* Strawberry Flavor Gelatin**

½ **cup cold orange-pineapple-banana juice**
    Ice cubes

1 **tub (8 ounces) COOL WHIP Whipped Topping, thawed, divided**

1 **prepared graham cracker crumb crust (6 ounce *or* 9 inch)**

1 **cup cut-up seasonal fruit**

Stir boiling juice into gelatin in large bowl at least 2 minutes until completely dissolved. Mix cold juice and ice to make 1 cup. Add to gelatin, stirring until slightly thickened. Remove any remaining ice.

Stir in 2½ cups of the whipped topping with wire whisk until smooth. Refrigerate 20 to 25 minutes or until mixture is very thick and will mound.

Spoon into crust. Refrigerate 4 hours or overnight. Just before serving, top with fruit and remaining whipped topping. Store leftover pie in refrigerator.

Summer LEM'N BERRY SIPPERS® Pie

Prep time: 15 minutes plus freezing

Makes 8 servings

COUNTRY TIME LEM'N BERRY SIPPERS Drink Mix, any flavor, *or* COUNTRY TIME Lemonade Flavor Drink Mix

½ **cup water**

1 **pint (2 cups) strawberry *or* raspberry sorbet, softened**

1 **tub (8 ounces) COOL WHIP Whipped Topping, thawed**

1 **prepared graham cracker crumb crust (6 ounce *or* 9 inch)**

Measure drink mix into cap just to 1-quart line. Stir drink mix and water in large bowl until dissolved.

Beat in sorbet with electric mixer on low speed until well blended. Gently stir in whipped topping until smooth. Freeze 15 minutes or until mixture will mound.

Spoon into crust. Freeze 4 hours or overnight until firm. Let stand at room temperature 15 minutes or until pie can be cut easily. Garnish with blueberries, raspberries and sliced strawberries. Store leftover pie in freezer.

Creamy Chocolate Pie

Prep time: 10 minutes   Refrigerating time: 4 hours

Makes 8 servings

1¾ **cups cold milk**
2 **packages (4-serving size *each*) JELL-O Chocolate *or* Chocolate Fudge Flavor Instant Pudding & Pie Filling**
1 **tub (8 ounces) COOL WHIP Whipped Topping, thawed**
1 **prepared chocolate flavor crumb crust (6 ounce *or* 9 inch)**

Pour milk into large bowl. Add pudding mixes. Beat with wire whisk 2 minutes or until smooth. (Mixture will be thick.) Immediately stir in whipped topping. Spoon into crust.

Refrigerate 4 hours or until set. Garnish with additional whipped topping and grated BAKER'S Semi-Sweet Baking Chocolate. Store leftover pie in refrigerator.

Creamy Choose-a-Flavor Pie

Looking for an easy—and delicious—dessert? Just prepare Creamy Chocolate Pie as directed, substituting your favorite pudding flavor.

5 Minute Double *Layer Pie*

Prep time: 5 minutes plus refrigerating

Makes 8 servings

1¼ **cups cold milk**
2 **packages (4-serving size *each*) JELL-O Instant Pudding & Pie Filling, any flavor**
1 **tub (8 ounces) COOL WHIP Whipped Topping, thawed, divided**
1 **prepared graham cracker crumb crust (6 ounce *or* 9 inch)**

Pour milk into medium bowl. Add pudding mixes and ½ of the whipped topping. Beat with wire whisk 1 minute. (Mixture will be thick.) Spread in crust.

Spread remaining whipped topping over pudding layer in crust. Refrigerate until ready to serve. Garnish with multi-colored sprinkles. Store leftover pie in refrigerator.

5 Minute White Chocolate *Hazelnut* Pie

Prep time: 5 minutes plus refrigerating

Makes 8 servings

1¼   **cups cold milk**

2   **packages (4-serving size *each*) JELL-O White Chocolate Flavor Instant Pudding & Pie Filling *or* other Chocolate Flavor**

2   **tablespoons (0.64 ounce) GENERAL FOODS INTERNATIONAL COFFEES, hazelnut flavor *or* any other flavor**

1   **tub (8 ounces) COOL WHIP Whipped Topping, thawed, divided**

1   **prepared chocolate flavor crumb crust (6 ounce *or* 9 inch)**

Pour milk into medium bowl. Add pudding mixes, coffee and ½ of the whipped topping. Beat with wire whisk 1 minute. (Mixture will be thick.) Spread in crust.

Spread remaining whipped topping over pudding layer in crust. Refrigerate until ready to serve. Garnish as desired. Store leftover pie in refrigerator.

Instant Substitute

MAXWELL HOUSE Instant Coffee works well here, too. Prepare 5 Minute White Chocolate Hazelnut Pie as directed, substituting 2 to 3 teaspoons MAXWELL HOUSE Instant Coffee for GENERAL FOODS INTERNATIONAL COFFEES.

Strawberry Shortbread Pie

Prep time: 20 minutes   Refrigerating time: 3½ hours

Makes 8 servings

¾ **cup boiling water**
1 **package (3 ounces) JELL-O Brand Strawberry Flavor Gelatin**
¾ **cup cold water**
4 **ounces (½ of 8-ounce package) PHILADELPHIA Cream Cheese, softened**
1½ **cups thawed COOL WHIP Whipped Topping**
1 **cup diced strawberries**
1 **prepared shortbread pie crust (6 ounce or 9 inch)**

Stir boiling water into gelatin in large bowl at least 2 minutes until completely dissolved. Stir in cold water.

Beat cream cheese in large bowl with wire whisk until smooth. Gradually whisk in gelatin until well blended.

Place bowl of gelatin into larger bowl of ice and water. Let stand about 5 minutes, stirring often, until slightly thickened (consistency of unbeaten egg whites).

Stir in whipped topping with wire whisk until smooth. Stir in strawberries. Refrigerate 20 to 30 minutes or until mixture is very thick and will mound. Spoon into crust. Refrigerate 3 hours or until firm. Top with additional whipped topping and strawberry halves, if desired. Store leftover pie in refrigerator.

Frozen *Sorbet* Pie

Prep time: 15 minutes   Freezing time: 5 hours

Makes 8 servings

1   **pint (2 cups) strawberry *or* raspberry sorbet, softened**
1   **tub (8 ounces) COOL WHIP Whipped Topping, thawed, divided**
1   **prepared graham cracker crumb crust (6 ounce *or* 9 inch)**
1¼ **cups cold milk**
2   **packages (4-serving size *each*) JELL-O Vanilla Flavor Instant Pudding & Pie Filling**

Spoon sorbet into large bowl. Stir in ½ of the whipped topping until well blended. Spoon into crust. Place in freezer 1 hour or until slightly set.

Pour milk into large bowl. Add pudding mixes. Beat with wire whisk 2 minutes or until smooth. (Mixture will be thick.) Immediately stir in remaining whipped topping. Gently spoon over sorbet layer in crust.

Freeze 4 hours or overnight. To serve, let stand at room temperature or in refrigerator 15 minutes until pie can be cut easily. Garnish with additional whipped topping. Store leftover pie in freezer.

Take a Shortcut

To soften the sorbet for Frozen Sorbet Pie, heat it in microwave on MEDIUM (50%) for about 10 to 15 seconds.

Cheesecake Ice Cream *Dessert*

Prep time: 20 minutes   Freezing time: 4 hours

Makes 16 servings

1   **package (11.2 ounces) JELL-O No Bake Real Cheesecake**

2   **envelopes MAXWELL HOUSE Cafe Cappuccino** *or* **¼ cup GENERAL FOODS INTERNATIONAL COFFEES, Suisse Mocha Flavor, French Vanilla Cafe Flavor** *or* **Irish Cream Cafe Flavor**

2   **tablespoons sugar**

6   **tablespoons butter** *or* **margarine, melted**

1   **tablespoon water**

1½   **cups cold milk**

1   **tub (8 ounces) COOL WHIP Whipped Topping, thawed**
     Chocolate dessert topping

Line 9×5-inch loaf pan with foil, extending over edges to form handles.

Stir Crust Mix, instant flavored coffee, sugar, butter and water thoroughly in medium bowl until crumbs are well moistened. Press ½ cup of the mixture firmly onto bottom of prepared pan; reserve remaining crumb mixture.

Beat milk and Filling Mix in medium bowl with electric mixer on low speed until blended. Beat on medium speed 3 minutes. (Filling will be thick.) Gently stir in whipped topping.

Spoon ⅓ of the mixture over crust in pan. Top with ⅓ of the reserved crumb mixture; repeat layers. Cut through layers with knife or top of spoon several times to marbleize. Cover.

Freeze 4 hours or overnight. Lift from pan using foil as handles. Let stand at room temperature 10 minutes or until dessert can be cut easily. Garnish with raspberries. Serve with chocolate topping. Store leftover dessert in freezer.

Peanut Butter Loaf

Prep time: 15 minutes   Freezing time: 4 hours

Makes 8 to 10 servings

**1   package (16.1 ounces) JELL-O No Bake
      Peanut Butter Cup Dessert**
⅓   cup butter *or* margarine, melted
1⅓ cups cold milk

Place Topping Pouch in large bowl of boiling water; set aside. Line 9×5-inch loaf pan with foil, extending over edges to form handles. Stir Crust Mix and butter with fork in medium bowl until crumbs are well moistened. Press ½ of the crumbs firmly onto bottom of prepared pan; reserve remaining crumbs.

Pour cold milk into medium bowl. Add Filling Mix and Peanut Butter. Beat with electric mixer on lowest speed until blended. Beat on high speed 3 minutes. DO NOT UNDERBEAT. Spoon ½ of the filling mixture over crust in pan.

Remove pouch from water. Shake vigorously 60 seconds or until topping is no longer lumpy. Squeeze ½ of the topping over filling in pan. Set aside a little crumb mixture for garnish, if desired. Repeat layers with remaining crumbs, filling and topping. Freeze 4 hours or overnight. To serve, lift from pan to cutting board using foil as handles; remove foil. Let stand at room temperature 10 minutes for easier slicing. Sprinkle with reserved crumb mixture. Store leftover dessert in freezer.

ONE BOWL *Chocolate* Swirl Cheesecake

Prep time: 10 minutes plus refrigerating   Baking time: 40 minutes

Makes 8 servings

4   **squares BAKER'S Semi-Sweet Baking Chocolate**

2   **packages (8 ounces *each*) PHILADELPHIA Cream Cheese, softened, divided**

½   **cup sugar, divided**

2   **eggs, divided**

½   **teaspoon vanilla**

1   **purchased chocolate flavor *or* graham cracker crumb crust (6 ounce *or* 9 inch)**

Microwave chocolate in large microwavable bowl on HIGH 1½ to 2 minutes or until chocolate is almost melted, stirring halfway through heating time. Stir until chocolate is completely melted.

Beat 1 package of the cream cheese, ¼ cup of the sugar and 1 egg with electric mixer on medium speed until well blended. Gradually add melted chocolate until blended. Pour into crust. Beat remaining package cream cheese, sugar, egg and vanilla in same bowl until well blended. Spoon plain batter over chocolate batter. Swirl batters with knife several times for marble effect.

Bake at 350°F for 40 minutes or until center is almost set. Cool. Refrigerate 3 hours or overnight. Let stand at room temperature 20 minutes before serving. Garnish with fresh raspberries, if desired. Store leftover cheesecake in refrigerator.

Chocolate *Cherry* Cheesecake

Prep time: 15 minutes plus refrigerating

Makes 16 servings

2 **packages (21.4 ounces *each*) JELL-O No Bake Cherry *or* Strawberry Topped Cheesecake**

¼ **cup sugar**

¾ **cup (1½ sticks) butter *or* margarine, melted**

3 **cups cold milk**

3 **squares BAKER'S Semi-Sweet Baking Chocolate, melted and cooled**

Stir Crust Mixes, sugar, butter and 2 tablespoons water with fork in medium bowl until crumbs are well moistened. Firmly press ½ of the crumbs 2 inches up side of 9-inch springform pan. Press remaining crumbs firmly onto bottom, using measuring cup. Spoon 1 Fruit Pouch over crust.

Pour cold milk into large bowl. Add Filling Mixes. Beat with electric mixer on low speed until blended. Beat on medium speed 3 minutes. (Filling will be thick.) Immediately stir 1 cup cheesecake mixture into chocolate until smooth. Stir chocolate mixture into remaining cheesecake mixture until blended.

Spoon mixture over fruit in crust. Top with remaining Fruit Pouch. Refrigerate at least 1½ hours or until firm. To serve, run a small knife or spatula around side of pan to loosen crust; remove side of pan. Store leftover cheesecake in refrigerator.

Alternate Pan

No springform pan? Use a 13×9-inch pan for Chocolate Cherry Cheesecake. Just press all of the crumbs firmly onto the bottom of the pan. Continue as directed.

Fluffy 2-*Step* Cheesecake

Prep time: 15 minutes plus refrigerating

Makes 8 servings

1	**package (8 ounces) PHILADELPHIA Cream Cheese, softened**
⅓	**cup sugar**
1	**tub (8 ounces) COOL WHIP Whipped Topping, thawed**
1	**prepared graham cracker crumb crust (6 ounce *or* 9 inch)**

Beat cream cheese and sugar in large bowl with wire whisk or electric mixer until smooth. Gently stir in whipped topping.

Spoon into crust. Refrigerate 3 hours or until set. Garnish with thin apple slices and curled orange peel. Store leftover cheesecake in refrigerator.

Pudding Poke Brownies

Prep time: 30 minutes plus refrigerating   Baking time: 35 minutes

Makes 32

1   **package (19.8 ounces) brownie mix**
1½   **cups cold milk**
1   **package (4-serving size) JELL-O Vanilla Flavor Instant Pudding & Pie Filling**

Prepare and bake brownie mix as directed on package for 8- or 9-inch square baking pan. Remove from oven. Immediately use round handle of wooden spoon to poke holes at 1-inch intervals down through warm brownies to pan.

Pour cold milk into large bowl. Add pudding mix. Beat with wire whisk for 2 minutes. Quickly pour about ½ of the thin pudding mixture evenly over warm brownies and into holes. Tap pan lightly to fill holes. Let remaining pudding stand to thicken slightly. Spread remaining pudding over top of brownies to "frost" brownies.

Refrigerate 1 hour or until ready to serve. Cut into 2-inch squares. Cut each square diagonally into triangles. Store leftover brownies in refrigerator.

Raspberry Coconut Bars

Prep time: 15 minutes   Baking time: 45 minutes plus cooling

Makes 24

1¼ **cups flour**
¼ **teaspoon salt**
½ **cup (1 stick) butter *or* margarine, cut
    into chunks**
3 **tablespoons cold water**
2 **eggs**
½ **cup sugar**
2⅔ **cups (7 ounces) BAKER'S ANGEL FLAKE
    Coconut**
½ **cup red raspberry jam**

Mix flour and salt in medium bowl. Cut in butter until coarse crumbs form. Sprinkle water over mixture while tossing to blend well. Press evenly onto bottom of ungreased 9-inch square baking pan. Bake at 425°F for 20 minutes or until lightly browned. Remove pan from oven. Decrease oven temperature to 350°F.

Beat eggs in large bowl with electric mixer on high speed. Gradually add sugar, beating until thick and light in color. Stir in coconut. Spread jam over crust to within ¼ inch of edges. Carefully spread coconut mixture over jam.

Bake 25 minutes or until golden brown. Cool completely on wire rack. Cut into bars.

Chewy *Caramel* Bars

Prep time: 5 minutes plus refrigerating   Microwaving time: 3 minutes

Makes 32

8   cups POST GOLDEN CRISP Sweetened
     Puffed Wheat Cereal
1   cup peanuts
1   package (14 ounces) caramels,
     unwrapped
2   tablespoons water

Mix cereal and peanuts in large bowl.

Microwave caramels and water in microwavable bowl on HIGH 2 to 3 minutes or until caramels are melted and mixture is smooth, stirring every minute. Pour immediately over cereal mixture. Mix lightly until well coated.

Press firmly into greased 13×9-inch pan with lightly greased hands. Cool until firm; cut into bars. Store in tightly covered container.

COOL WHIP® *Smoothie*

Prep time: 5 minutes

Makes 2 servings

1 container (8 ounces) BREYERS Vanilla *or* Strawberry Lowfat Yogurt
1 cup thawed COOL WHIP Whipped Topping
1 cup chopped strawberries (optional)

Place yogurt, whipped topping and strawberries in blender container; cover. Blend until smooth. Serve immediately.

BREYERS is a registered trademark owned and licensed by Unilever, N.V.

Easy Sour Cream Fruit Topping

Prep time: 5 minutes plus refrigerating

Makes 1 cup

1 cup BREAKSTONE'S *or* KNUDSEN Sour Cream
2 tablespoons honey
1 tablespoon lemon juice

Mix ingredients. Refrigerate.

Spoon over assorted fresh berries. Garnish with fresh mint leaves.

Easy KOOL-AID® Snow Cones

Prep time: 5 minutes

Makes 8 servings

1 cup sugar
1 envelope KOOL-AID Unsweetened Soft
    Drink Mix, any flavor
½ cup cold water
8 cups finely crushed ice

Place sugar and soft drink mix in small plastic or glass bowl. Add water; stir to dissolve.

Pour about 1 tablespoon soft drink mixture over 1 cup ice. Serve immediately. Repeat with remaining soft drink mixture and ice.

Shortcut KOOL-AID® Snow Cones

Prepare Easy KOOL-AID® Snow Cones as directed, substituting ¾ cup KOOL-AID Sugar-Sweetened Soft Drink Mix, any flavor, for unsweetened soft drink mix. Omit sugar.

dessert *ideas*

*A sweet tooth doesn't take a summer vacation,
but you can. Just try these no-sweat, nifty, sweet ideas.*

**Fresh
Berry Cones**

Stir assorted fresh
berries into thawed
COOL WHIP
Whipped Topping.
Spoon into sugar
cones.

**Banana Split
Pudding Cones**

Spoon JELL-O Chocolate
Pudding Snack into sugar
cones. Top with thawed
COOL WHIP Whipped
Topping, sliced banana,
chopped nuts and maraschino
cherries.

Chocolate-Dipped Cones

Melt BAKER'S Semi-Sweet
Baking Chocolate in microwave
until almost melted,
stirring occasionally.
Remove from oven;
stir until completely
melted. Dip the edge
of each sugar cone into
the chocolate and let
the excess drip off. Let the
dipped cones stand, or
refrigerate them, until the
chocolate is firm. Fill with
ice cream and candies.

**Crunchy
Ice Cream Balls**

Roll scoops of ice cream in
lightly crushed cereal, such as
POST ALPHA-BITS Frosted Letter
Shaped Oat and Corn Cereal
or POST GOLDEN CRISP
Sweetened Puffed Wheat
Cereal. Freeze until firm.

GRILLING BASICS

Grilling seems to be just about everyone's favorite method of warm-weather cooking. To ensure great results every time, use these hints and timing guidelines.

BEFORE YOU GRILL

With a few grilling tools and a little preparation, grilling is a snap.

■ Assemble a "tool kit" consisting of long-handled tongs, spatulas, basting brushes, oven mitts and an instant-read thermometer so you know the meat is done just right.

■ Clean the grill rack thoroughly with a wire brush or crumpled foil before—and after—each use, to keep food from sticking.

■ To prevent foods from sticking to the grill rack during cooking, spray the unheated rack, away from the fire, with no stick cooking spray or brush with oil.

FIRE UP THE GRILL

Use these pointers to make sure that your charcoal or gas grill is the right temperature for cooking your food.

■ To light coals, heap them in the center of the grill and light them about 30 minutes before you need to start grilling.

■ After about 20 to 30 minutes, the coals should have gray ash on the outside, with no black showing. Inside they should glow red.

■ For direct grilling, arrange the hot coals in a single layer about ½ inch apart. Test the temperature of the coals by holding your hand 6 inches above the coals while slowly counting. When you need to remove your hand from the heat after 3 seconds, the coals are hot; after 4 seconds, they are medium-hot.

■ For gas grilling, set the burner to high. Light the master burner, then the other burners. Preheat about 15 minutes.

GRILLING MADE EASY

Once your grill reaches the temperature you want, you are ready to grill your food. For perfect cooking:

■ Space foods at least ¾ inch apart to allow for even cooking.

■ Use tongs or a metal spatula to move and turn meat on the grill, rather than using a fork. Piercing the meat with a fork causes the juices to escape, which makes the meat less flavorful and less moist.

■ Cover the grill when grilling to prevent flare-ups and charring of meat, and to help it cook evenly.

GRILLING TIMES

Forget guessing how long dinner will take on the grill—now you can see at a glance. Follow the timings at right and use an instant-read thermometer to check the doneness, making sure the center reaches the recommended temperature.

For meat:

Grill, uncovered, directly over medium coals for the time suggested at right or until recommended doneness, turning halfway through.

Cut of meat	Thickness	Doneness	Time
Beef steak	1 inch	Medium (160°F)	12 to 15 minutes
Flank steak	¾ to 1 inch	Medium (160°F)	12 to 14 minutes
Meat patties	¾ inch	No pink left (160°F)	14 to 18 minutes
Pork chop	1¼ inches	Well (170°F)	25 to 30 minutes
Pork chop	½ inch	Well (170°F)	14 to 16 minutes
Frankfurters	5 to 6 per pound	Hot (160°F)	5 to 8 minutes
Kabobs	1-inch cubes	Medium (160°F)	12 to 14 minutes

For poultry:

Remove the skin, if desired. Rinse and pat dry with paper towels. Grill, uncovered, directly over medium coals for the time suggested at right or until tender and no longer pink.

Type of bird	Weight	Doneness	Time
Chicken breast half, skinned and boned	4 to 5 ounces	160°F	12 to 15 minutes
Ground turkey patties	¾ inch	165°F	14 to 18 minutes

For fish:

Thaw fish if frozen. Place in a well-greased wire basket or grease the grill rack. Grill, uncovered, directly over medium coals for the time suggested at right or until the fish flakes when you test it with a fork.

Form of fish	Thickness	Time
Fillets	½ inch	4 to 6 minutes
Steaks or kabobs	1 inch	8 to 12 minutes

For vegetables:

Rinse, trim and cut up vegetables as directed. Generously brush vegetables with olive oil, margarine or butter before grilling to prevent vegetables from sticking to the grill rack. Place vegetables on a piece of heavy foil or on the grill rack directly over medium coals. If putting vegetables directly on grill rack, lay them perpendicular to the wires of the rack so they won't fall into the coals. Grill, uncovered, for the time suggested at right or until tender, turning occasionally and watching for charring.

Vegetable	Preparation	Time
Bell peppers	Remove stems. Quarter peppers. Remove seeds and membranes. Cut into 1-inch-wide strips.	8 to 10 minutes
Eggplant	Cut off top and blossom ends. Cut eggplant crosswise into 1-inch-thick slices.	8 minutes
Zucchini or yellow summer squash	Wash; cut off ends. Quarter lengthwise.	5 to 6 minutes

METRIC COOKING HINTS

By making a few conversions, cooks in Australia, Canada and the United Kingdom can use the recipes in this book with confidence. The charts on this page provide a guide for converting measurements from the U.S. customary system, which is used throughout this book, to the imperial and metric systems. There also is a conversion table for oven temperatures to accommodate the differences in oven calibrations.

Product Differences: Most of the ingredients called for in the recipes in this book are available in English-speaking countries. However, some are known by different names. Here are some common U.S. American ingredients and their possible counterparts:

- Sugar is granulated or castor sugar.
- Powdered sugar is icing sugar.
- Flour is plain household flour or white flour. When self-rising flour is used in place of all-purpose flour in a recipe that calls for leavening, omit the leavening agent (baking soda or baking powder) and salt.
- Light corn syrup is golden syrup.
- Cornstarch is cornflour.
- Baking soda is bicarbonate of soda.
- Vanilla is vanilla essence.
- Green, red or yellow peppers are capsicums.
- Golden raisins are sultanas.

Volume and Weight: U.S. Americans traditionally use cup measures for liquid and solid ingredients. The chart, below, shows the approximate imperial and metric equivalents. If you are accustomed to weighing solid ingredients, the following approximate equivalents will help.

- 1 cup butter, castor sugar or rice = 8 ounces = about 230 grams
- 1 cup flour = 4 ounces = about 115 grams
- 1 cup icing sugar = 5 ounces = about 140 grams

Spoon measures are used for smaller amounts of ingredients. Although the size of the tablespoon varies slightly in different countries, for practical purposes and for recipes in this book, a straight substitution is all that's necessary.

Measurements made using cups or spoons always should be level unless stated otherwise.

EQUIVALENTS: U.S. = AUSTRALIA/U.K.

1/5 teaspoon = 1 ml	1/2 cup = 120 ml
1/4 teaspoon = 1.25 ml	2/3 cup = 160 ml
1/2 teaspoon = 2.5 ml	3/4 cup = 180 ml
1 teaspoon = 5 ml	1 cup = 240 ml
1 tablespoon = 15 ml	2 cups = 475 ml
1 fluid ounce = 30 ml	1 quart = 1 liter
1/4 cup = 60 ml	1/2 inch = 1.25 cm
1/3 cup = 80 ml	1 inch = 2.5 cm

BAKING PAN SIZES

U.S.	Metric
8×1½-inch round baking pan	20×4-cm cake tin
9×1½-inch round baking pan	23×4-cm cake tin
11×7×1½-inch baking pan	28×18×4-cm baking tin
13×9×2-inch baking pan	32×23×5-cm baking tin
2-quart rectangular baking dish	28×18×4-cm baking tin
15×10×1-inch baking pan	38×25.5×2.5-cm baking tin (Swiss roll tin)
9-inch pie plate	22×4- or 23×4-cm pie plate
7- or 8-inch springform pan	18- or 20-cm springform or loose-bottom cake tin
9×5×3-inch loaf pan	23×13×8-cm or 2-pound narrow loaf tin or pâté tin
1½-quart casserole	1.5-liter casserole
2-quart casserole	2-liter casserole

OVEN TEMPERATURE EQUIVALENTS

Fahrenheit Setting	Celsius Setting*	Gas Setting
300°F	150°C	Gas mark 2 (very low)
325°F	170°C	Gas mark 3 (low)
350°F	180°C	Gas mark 4 (moderate)
375°F	190°C	Gas mark 5 (moderately hot)
400°F	200°C	Gas mark 6 (hot)
425°F	220°C	Gas mark 7 (hot)
450°F	230°C	Gas mark 8 (very hot)
475°F	240°C	Gas mark 9 (very hot)
Broil		Grill

*Electric and gas ovens may be calibrated using Celsius. However, for an electric oven, increase the Celsius setting 10 to 20 degrees when cooking above 160°C. For convection or forced-air ovens (gas or electric), lower the temperature setting 10°C when cooking at all heat levels.